I0530006

DRIVE SAFELY PUBLISHING

A Complete Driving Guide for Seniors

Practical Guidance on Planning Ahead, Staying Alert, and Arriving Safely to Your Destination

Contents

1

Copyright © 2025 by Drive Safely Publishing

All trademarks, service marks, product names, or brand names mentioned in this book are the property of their respective owners and are used only in an educational context. No endorsement by, or affiliation with, those entities is implied.

The guidance provided in this book does not replace official laws, regulations, or professional advice from medical providers, licensing authorities, or certified driving instructors. Always consult qualified professionals when making decisions about health, driving ability, or legal requirements.

2

Disclaimer

This book is intended solely as an educational resource to support safe driving habits among senior drivers. It is not a substitute for professional medical advice, legal guidance, or official recommendations from state licensing authorities, law enforcement, or certified driving specialists.

Every driver's situation is unique. Age, health conditions, medications, physical abilities, and personal driving history all play a role in determining whether it is safe to continue driving. Readers are strongly encouraged to consult with their healthcare providers, vision specialists, or other qualified professionals regarding any physical or medical concerns that may affect their driving ability.

While this guide offers strategies, tools, and knowledge to promote safety and independence, driving always involves risks. Road conditions, weather, traffic, and other unpredictable factors can create situations beyond the scope of this book. Ultimately, each driver is responsible for assessing their own ability, making sound decisions behind the wheel, and complying with all applicable traffic laws and regulations.

The author and publisher disclaim any liability for accidents, injuries, damages, or other consequences that may result from the use or misuse of the information contained in this book.

3

Introduction

On a bright Saturday morning, Edna steps out her door, keys in hand. She drives to her daughter's house, shops for fresh oranges, and visits the community garden. These trips are more than errands—they are acts of independence, giving her freedom, purpose, and connection.

For many seniors, driving is not just transportation. It is autonomy, dignity, and the link to family, friends, and community. Yet, it's normal to feel concern about vision changes, slower reflexes, or the effects of medication. You may even worry about losing your license and relying on others.

This guide is here to help you. My goal is not to take away your keys, but to give you tools to keep driving safely for as long as possible. Safe driving is about adapting, building smart habits, and knowing your limits while maintaining independence.

As a certified driving instructor with 17 years of experience, I have worked with many seniors who want to stay safe and confident on the road. In this book, we'll cover how aging affects driving, ways to plan trips, stay alert, manage tricky situations, and keep your vehicle in top shape. We'll also look at alternatives like ride services and community shuttles that can help you stay mobile when needed.

Driving safely as a senior is about more than following rules—it's about protecting your freedom and staying connected. Use this book as a trusted resource whenever you need guidance or reassurance. Together, we'll keep you safely on the road, enjoying every journey ahead.

4

Chapter 1: Embracing the Road Ahead: Driving as Independence and Connection

You might remember the familiar feeling of turning the key on a crisp morning, the quiet rumble of the engine hinting at a day shaped by your own choices. Maybe it's a basket of groceries on the passenger seat after a market trip, or pulling into the church lot early to share a few words with friends. These small, everyday drives carry meaning far beyond the road itself—they reflect freedom, routine, and the joy of staying connected.

Driving and Aging—Staying Connected, Staying Free

Driving is more than a way to get from your home to the store or doctor's office—it's a bridge to the world outside your front door. It allows you to visit grandchildren, pick up prescriptions, or make a quick stop for dinner ingredients without depending on anyone else. These everyday errands, simple as they seem, carry pride and meaning. They let you manage your own needs on your own schedule, reinforcing dignity, confidence, and independence.

Driving is also a powerful way to maintain social connection. It means showing up at community gatherings, weekly bridge games, Rotary meetings, or volunteer events. Friendships grow by being present, and driving makes that possible. Staying active in your community supports not just your relationships but also your mental health and happiness. Research shows that seniors who stay engaged in social life often feel less isolated and maintain better overall well-being.

There's also a link between mobility and mental sharpness. Outings expose you to new sights, conversations, and experiences that lift your mood and keep your mind active. Even a slow drive through a park or down familiar back roads can spark joy and reflection. Having the option to say "yes" to coffee with a friend or an evening play is a freedom that matters deeply.

It's natural, then, to feel anxious about losing that independence. The idea of handing over your keys can feel unsettling, even unfair. Many worry that without driving, their world will shrink and their connections will fade. These feelings are valid. You are not alone in them. My goal in this guide is to help you extend your driving years safely, so you can continue enjoying the benefits of staying behind the wheel.

Consider Marie, who every Wednesday picks up her granddaughter from preschool for ice cream and an afternoon together. She treasures those drives not only for the laughter but because she knows her family counts on her. Or Harold, who meets friends at the café every Saturday. He once said, "Driving is more than my license—it's my place in their lives." For many seniors, it's exactly that: the key to staying connected, valued, and independent.

Reflect: What Does Driving Mean To You?

Take a moment to consider what being able to drive means in your daily life. Think about the people you visit, the places you go, and the way you feel when you're able to decide your own schedule. If you'd like, jot down a few of these thoughts in a notebook or on a sheet at the end of this chapter. Noticing what matters most will help us focus on keeping those parts of your life strong and supported as we move forward.

Driving is about much more than steering a vehicle—it's about maintaining ties with loved ones, nurturing independence, and staying engaged with your community. It supports not just your physical mobility but your emotional well-being. This guide exists not to take away these important things but to help you preserve them as long as possible—safely, confidently, and with dignity.

Overcoming Fear—Addressing the Emotional Side of Driving Change

Aging brings a wide range of emotions, especially when it comes to driving. You may notice anxiety before a trip, pride in your years of safe driving, and quiet questions about safety all at once. Thoughts like "Am I still safe?" or "Will my family worry if I mention a close call?" can linger, especially as changes in vision, reaction time, or comfort on busy roads become more noticeable.

Denial often plays a role too. It's easy to dismiss mistakes as flukes or blame the other driver, since driving has always felt second nature. But admitting that things are changing isn't defeat—it's honesty, and you're not alone in it. Many seniors share this tug-of-war between holding onto independence and quietly questioning their safety.

These emotions run deeper than simple frustration. Driving connects strongly to identity—freedom, contribution, and belonging. Needing more time at intersections, feeling anxious on highways, or avoiding night driving can stir feelings of loss, even when the adjustment is wise.

Anxiety over safety is normal and can even be healthy—it means you care about protecting yourself and others. Still, constant worry can turn driving into stress or avoidance. One way to regain calm is to prepare before each trip: adjust your seat and mirrors, review your route, and be sure you're well-rested. These simple steps help boost focus and confidence.

Pride matters too. Determination helps keep you active, but pride can also suggest that asking for help means giving up. In truth, seeking guidance or making adjustments shows strength. It reflects a commitment to making safe choices, even when they're difficult.

Family plays a role as well. Sharing your concerns doesn't mean giving up control. Framing it as an invitation for ideas—such as, "I'm noticing it's harder to see road signs at night—do you have any suggestions?"—keeps the conversation collaborative instead of judgmental.

Finally, calming strategies can make stressful drives easier. Deep breathing at a red light, repeating a reassuring phrase like "Take it slow, stay alert," or keeping a small calming object nearby can all help. The goal isn't to erase nerves but to manage them so you feel steady and in control.

Pre-Drive Confidence Checklist

Before each trip, go through this list:

- Did I sleep well last night?
- Have I taken any new medications today?
- Are my glasses clean and up to date?
- Do I feel steady on my feet?
- Is my route familiar?
- Is there bad weather I should prepare for?
- Have I told someone where I'm going if the drive is long?

Checking these boxes isn't about doubt—it's about setting yourself up for success and peace of mind.

The stigma around asking for help is real, but it doesn't have to control your choices. Adjustments like adding a cushion for back support, using larger dashboard buttons, or updating your glasses prescription aren't admissions of defeat—they're smart steps for anyone who values their safety and independence. If talking with a neighbor who's gone through similar changes helps you feel less alone, reach out. If taking a refresher driving course boosts your comfort level, sign up without hesitation (AARP, n.d.). Each small act of preparation is an act of strength.

Change always brings mixed emotions—fear, pride, sadness, hope—but facing those feelings honestly is what keeps you safe and in charge of your own life.

What Safe Driving Really Means for Seniors

Safe driving as you age isn't about shrinking your world or giving up what you enjoy—it's about driving smarter. That means making choices that protect you and those around you while allowing you to keep your independence. Safety doesn't mean surrendering the driver's seat; it means adapting. The road may look different at 75 than it did at 45, but good driving is built on more than reflexes—it comes from years of judgment, awareness, and respect for your own limits.

Driving smarter is an active process. Vision and hearing naturally change over time, but small adjustments make a big difference. Regular eye exams, anti-glare or night-driving glasses, and audiology checks can sharpen your senses. Even turning down the radio helps you catch important sounds like sirens or horns.

Fatigue is another factor to watch. Sleep patterns shift with age, and some medications can cause drowsiness. Rest before driving, plan shorter trips, and avoid heavy traffic when you know you'll be more alert. If medications affect your focus, talk with your doctor or pharmacist about alternatives.

Physical comfort matters, too. Arthritis can make gripping the wheel or pressing pedals uncomfortable, but steering wheel covers, pedal extenders, seat cushions, and wide-angle mirrors can restore ease and confidence. Technology like backup cameras can reduce stress in parking lots, while larger dashboard controls or adaptive features make vehicles easier to manage.

These changes aren't limitations—they're tools. A woman I knew extended the life of her favorite sedan for years with nothing more than a seat cushion and mirror attachments. Simple fixes often make driving not only possible but more comfortable than before.

The truth is, most seniors who continue to drive safely do so by adapting, not by doing less. They act early, make small adjustments, and use their wisdom to stay ahead of challenges.

Throughout this guide, you'll find checklists covering everything from tire pressure to medication timing. Keep one in your glove box or near the garage door for quick reference. Each step is a way of taking control, reinforcing that safe driving is about strength, not loss.

Being a safe senior driver means embracing change with confidence. It's about knowing your abilities, recognizing challenges, and using every available resource—whether it's a new pair of glasses, updated technology, or a simple checklist—to keep you independent and secure on the road.

Meeting Common Objections—This Isn't About Taking Away Your Keys

When I meet with older drivers, the same questions often come up: "I already know how to drive—what's new here?" or "Is this just going to tell me to stop driving?" These concerns come from decades of experience and confidence behind the wheel, as well as frustration with resources that rush seniors toward giving up. If you've been driving a lifetime, you don't want a stranger telling you it's time to quit.

Let's be clear: this guide isn't about taking away your keys or independence. It's about helping you continue driving safely, for as long as possible, on your terms. I'm not here to scold or force decisions. Instead, I share strategies and insights that strengthen your skills and keep you confident behind the wheel.

Some believe nothing new can be learned after years of driving. But everything changes—roads, vehicles, and our own bodies. Great drivers stay adaptable. This guide blends wisdom from seniors, expert advice, and real-world stories that speak directly to the challenges you may face: how medications affect reflexes, how car technology improves safety, and how simple checklists can make driving easier.

The fear that "this book will just tell me to stop driving" is common. Many resources for seniors emphasize restrictions, leaving drivers feeling pressured. This book is different. I believe most seniors can drive safely far longer with honest information and practical strategies. My goal is to extend your safe driving years so that, if you ever reduce your driving, it's by choice—not demand.

You'll also find stories from peers who discovered simple changes that made a big impact. George, a retired teacher, doubted he'd learn anything new about car technology. But one page on mirror adjustment changed his daily driving—he stopped straining his neck and began driving with more ease. He still keeps that page in his car as proof that learning never really stops.

Expert input also shapes this guide. Occupational therapists and physicians who specialize in aging contributed insights on vision, reaction time, and safe habits. As Dr. Linda Beckwith, a geriatrician, explains: "The seniors who stay behind the wheel longest are those who stay curious, open to changes, and willing to use new tools." That spirit guides this book.

Some drivers feel overwhelmed by today's vehicle features, but this guide breaks them down clearly, with plain-language explanations and step-by-step illustrations. Whether it's using a backup camera or adjusting your seat, no tech expertise is required.

It's natural to think, "But I've always done it this way." Habits are hard to change. Yet traffic, weather, and even familiar routes evolve. Safe driving isn't about clinging to old methods—it's about adapting to today's conditions.

Throughout these pages, you'll also find stories from seniors who overcame setbacks, whether it was a small accident that shook their confidence or a health event that forced adjustments. Their experiences show that setbacks don't have to end your driving—they can open the door to safer, smarter habits.

Every tool, tip, and checklist in this guide has worked for someone like you. Even one small change might make driving tomorrow easier, or give you the words to start a productive conversation with your doctor or family. And if all you take away is reassurance that you're already doing your best, that alone is valuable.

This book isn't about losing independence—it's about protecting it, on your terms, at your pace.

How to Use This Guide as Your Personal Roadmap

Think of this book as a toolkit you can reach for whenever you need support behind the wheel. Each chapter focuses on a different topic, moving from how aging affects driving to practical habits, vehicle adjustments, and even ways to stay connected if you decide to drive less.

At the end of most sections, you'll find "check-in questions." These aren't tests, but prompts to reflect on your own habits. For example, after reading about planning safe routes, you might ask, "Do I usually avoid driving at dusk?" Write your thoughts in the margins, a notebook, or simply say them out loud. The goal is to pause, reflect, and stay aware of your own patterns.

This isn't a book for passive reading. Treat it as interactive. Fill out the checklists, try the exercises in your own car, and mark the tips that matter most to you. Discuss sections with a spouse, friend, or family member if you're noticing changes in your confidence or comfort on the road.

The guide addresses both the practical and emotional sides of senior driving. You'll find advice on safe habits, technology that makes driving easier, and strategies for managing stress or discussing concerns with family. Safe driving is about more than the car itself—it's also about supporting your confidence and peace of mind.

Keep this book handy. Glance at it before an unfamiliar drive, after a near-miss, or when considering a new medication. Use it in small bursts—review car maintenance one week, family conversations the next—or revisit the checklists before a trip. It's a flexible resource meant to grow with you.

You may find it especially useful during transitions, like preparing for a road trip, renewing your license, or discussing concerns with loved ones. Setting aside even ten minutes a week to review a checklist or section can make safe habits second nature. And when you face something unfamiliar, remind yourself—learning is always possible at any age.

Above all, remember this guide is yours to use however you choose. It's here to keep you driving with confidence, comfort, and peace of mind—no matter where the road leads.

5

Chapter 2: Understanding How Aging Affects Your Driving

Vision Changes—Spotting Hazards and Managing Glare

Picture heading out for a morning drive: sunlight filters through the trees and suddenly glare makes it hard to see the car ahead. You squint at a sign, struggling to read it. If this feels familiar, you're not alone. Aging naturally affects how our eyes work on the road. It's not a sign of failure—it's simply part of getting older. By understanding common vision changes and knowing how to adapt, you can stay safer and more confident behind the wheel.

Several age-related eye conditions can influence driving. Cataracts create cloudy patches in the lens, making things look hazy, like peering through frosted glass. Glaucoma narrows your field of vision, making cyclists or merging cars easier to miss. Presbyopia affects near vision, complicating quick glances at your dashboard or map. Macular degeneration reduces central vision, making it harder to read signs. These changes often appear gradually, so you may not notice them until traffic lights, curbs, or pedestrians feel harder to spot.

Contrast sensitivity also declines with age, which makes it harder to distinguish objects from their background—like faded lane markings in the rain or white letters on a green street sign. Night vision can fade too, leading to halos or starbursts around headlights that make night or wet-weather driving more stressful.

Fortunately, there are practical ways to improve what you see. Polarized sunglasses reduce daytime reflections from wet pavement, windshields, or low winter sun. Anti-glare visors or windshield films can soften harsh light without making things too dark. Always use your car's built-in visor for low sun, and avoid placing shiny objects on your dashboard that may reflect into your eyes.

Cleanliness matters too. Dust and streaks on your windshield or mirrors scatter light and intensify glare. Before driving, wipe both sides of your windshield with a microfiber cloth (not paper towels, which leave lint). Clean your mirrors and headlights as well—dirty headlights can reduce nighttime visibility by up to 30%. Adjust your mirrors so they show the road while minimizing blind spots, setting them outward until just the edge of your car is visible.

In addition to sunglasses and clean windshields, a few simple upgrades can make driving easier on the eyes. Clip-on visor extenders or tinted side panels help block the low morning or evening sun that factory visors often miss. If you wear glasses, ask your eye doctor about anti-reflective coatings and be sure to keep lenses spotless—small smudges can magnify glare, especially with bifocals or readers.

Before any evening drive, do a quick "visibility check." Walk around your car and make sure headlights, taillights, and brake lights are clean and bright. Wipe off the dashboard display inside, since dust can reflect light into your eyes at night. These small habits reduce strain and improve comfort for both daytime glare and nighttime driving.

At-Home Vision Self-Check Exercise

You can do a simple vision check at home to test how well you read roadside signs at a distance. Write or print common signs—like "Stop," "Yield," or "Speed Limit 25"—in large letters and tape them to a wall. From the end of a hallway, see how far away you can read each one. Try it in daylight, at dusk, and under indoor lighting. If you struggle—especially in dim light or if the letters blur—it's time to schedule an eye exam.

Regular eye exams are essential, even if you think your vision hasn't changed. After age 65, most experts recommend seeing an eye doctor every one to two years. Between visits, pay attention to new difficulties, such as night driving, reading signs, or adjusting between bright and dim conditions. Many pharmacies also offer quick screening tools if you want a simple check in between appointments.

A few car adjustments can also make driving easier on your eyes. Keep lens wipes in your glove box for quick cleaning. Add wide-angle mirrors if turning your head is uncomfortable—they expand your field of view with little effort. Use clear dashboard covers so warning lights and displays stay easy to read.

With regular eye care and these small adjustments, you'll keep your vision sharper and your driving safer.

Hearing and Sound Cues on the Road

Hearing plays a bigger role in driving than many realize. Sirens, horns, the click of a turn signal, or the rumble of a motorcycle all provide vital cues about what's happening beyond your line of sight. As we age, hearing changes can make these sounds harder to notice. High-pitched tones often fade first— you may find voices muffled, need the TV louder, or miss the sound of an ambulance approaching from behind.

Age-related hearing loss, or presbycusis, usually develops gradually. You may not realize you've missed a warning beep or another car's horn until later. This isn't just inconvenient—it can be dangerous, especially in heavy traffic where sound alerts are critical. For some, hearing aids help, but background noise inside the car can blur important signals.

There are practical steps to stay tuned in. If you wear hearing aids, check them before each drive and keep extra batteries in your glove box. Adjust settings for "noisy environments" if available. Turn down or mute the radio, since music can cover subtle cues like sirens. If you normally drive with windows open, consider keeping them up in busy traffic to reduce outside clatter. Experiment with what setup helps you focus best.

Developing habits that sharpen sound awareness is also useful. Before driving, run a quick "sound check" in your parked car:

- Turn on your blinker—can you hear the click?
- Buckle and unbuckle your seatbelt—does the chime sound?
- Tap the horn—does the tone come through clearly?
- Start the engine—do you hear any dashboard alerts?

If one of these is faint or missing, it may be time to check your hearing or service your car's alert systems.

You can also ask family or friends to ride along and notice if you miss cues. Or try a simple at-home test: sit in your car with eyes closed while someone outside makes different noises—a bike bell, a horn, or a knock on the window—and see which you detect.

Regular audiologist visits are just as important as eye exams. Specialists can run driver-focused tests and may recommend programmable hearing aids designed for in-car acoustics. Addressing hearing loss early helps protect both independence and safety.

Modern vehicles also provide backup support. Many display flashing dashboard lights when another car is in your blind spot or if a door isn't fully closed. Backup sensors and cross-traffic alerts use beeps, vibrations, or even blinking lights that can be adjusted to your needs. Older vehicles can often be fitted with aftermarket visual alert systems.

By staying aware of hearing changes and making small adjustments, you keep pace with traffic's demands. Driving isn't just about seeing the road—it's about listening to it, too.

Reflexes and Reaction Time—Simple Exercises to Stay Sharp

Have you noticed it sometimes takes longer to react when the car ahead brakes suddenly, or that merging onto a busy highway feels faster than your hands and feet can respond? These moments are common with age. Slower reflexes and longer reaction times can slip in gradually, often showing up only during a close call. A one-second delay may not sound like much, but on the road it can mean braking too late or hesitating when you need to act quickly. This isn't a personal failing—it's simply how the body and mind change over time.

The good news: you can train your reflexes to stay sharper. A few daily exercises help your brain and body work together more efficiently. Try the "light switch drill"—flip light switches on and off quickly as you walk through your home, alternating hands. It boosts hand-eye coordination in a simple way. Another is the ball toss exercise. Toss a tennis ball with a partner or bounce it against a wall, catching it with alternating hands. Gradually increase speed. Both drills wake up reflexes, improve coordination, and are easy to fit into your day.

Physical activity also supports quicker reactions. You don't need intense workouts—gentle routines that keep joints flexible and muscles active are enough. Chair yoga, morning stretches, walking, or swimming all help. The more limber you are, the easier it is to move from gas to brake or turn the wheel without hesitation.

You can also practice reaction skills right in your car—safely, with the engine off. Sit in the driver's seat and rest your right foot flat on the floor. Move it quickly to the brake pedal as if responding to an emergency. Use a stopwatch or phone timer and repeat the drill five times. If you notice slower movements than before, or if it feels awkward, consider adding more daily exercises or discussing ways to improve mobility with your doctor.

Self-Assessment Checklist: Are My Reflexes Slowing?

Take a few minutes with this checklist before your next drive:

- Do I need more time than usual to step on the brake in unexpected situations?
- Have I hesitated merging into traffic because I wasn't sure I could move fast enough?
- Am I slow to react when a light turns green or when pedestrians step into the crosswalk?
- Do I struggle to quickly turn my head or hands when backing out of a parking spot?
- Have family members commented on my response time?

If you check off two or more items, consider making reflex exercises part of your daily habit. It's never too late to improve speed and coordination. Small steps can add up quickly—and even bring some fun back into staying sharp for the road.

Medication and Driving—The Hidden Risks

Many common medications can quietly affect driving. Blood pressure drugs, sleep aids, and painkillers may cause drowsiness, dizziness, or slower reflexes—even if you've taken them for years. As we age, the body processes medicine differently, so side effects often become stronger. Even over-the-counter remedies like allergy pills or cold medicine can cause grogginess or delayed reaction times.

Mixing medications increases these risks. Combining prescriptions for pain, blood sugar, and sleep may create unexpected side effects, leaving you sluggish or less alert than you realize. Sometimes the danger isn't clear until after a close call or an episode of sudden drowsiness. Because symptoms develop gradually, it's easy to dismiss fatigue as poor sleep or blame dizziness on dehydration.

One of the best safety steps is to keep a written list of every medication you take, including vitamins and supplements. Carry it in your wallet or glove box and show it to your doctor or pharmacist whenever a new prescription is added. Ask directly: "Could this affect my driving or alertness?" Pharmacists, in particular, are skilled at spotting risky interactions.

When starting a new medicine or adjusting a dose, consider a short "test drive" with a co-pilot—a spouse, friend, or adult child—on familiar, low-traffic roads. Pay attention to how you feel, and ask your passenger if they notice changes in your driving. They may see things you don't.

Tracking your reactions is also valuable. Keep a small journal where you record when you take each pill, how you feel 30 minutes later, and any symptoms like sleepiness, dizziness, or fuzzy thinking. Over time, this can help you and your doctor identify which medications affect you most.

Prepare focused questions before talking to your doctor or pharmacist:

· Can this cause drowsiness or slower reactions?
· Will it interact with my current medications?
· Should I avoid driving until I know how it affects me?

Reactions to medicine vary, and what felt harmless at 55 can have stronger effects at 75. The body metabolizes drugs more slowly with age, which means side effects may last longer. Even small changes—like skipping a meal or driving in hot weather—can make the impact worse.

Using a structured medication checklist helps. Write down each pill and supplement, noting the name, dose, and time taken. Mark those known to cause drowsiness or dizziness. Track how you feel afterward and review this list regularly with your medical team.

Talking about medication and driving may feel uncomfortable, but being open with your care providers protects both your safety and your independence. By monitoring closely and asking questions, you can stay alert, confident, and behind the wheel for longer.

Managing Stiffness, Pain, and Limited Mobility Behind the Wheel

For many seniors, stiffness and pain are more than annoyances—they can shape every part of a drive. Arthritis or sore joints make simple actions harder: turning to check blind spots, getting in and out of the car, or gripping the wheel for long periods. You might even avoid trips because driving feels uncomfortable. These challenges are common, but they don't have to keep you from driving safely.

Joint pain often shows up in ways you don't expect. Turning your neck to look over your shoulder may feel restricted. Reaching for the seatbelt can cause discomfort. Holding the steering wheel may leave your hands sore or numb, and pressing pedals can be awkward if hips or knees resist bending. Over time, these small difficulties can affect reaction time or cause you to miss what's happening outside the car.

Fortunately, many car accessories can make driving easier. Soft steering wheel covers reduce strain on stiff fingers. Swivel seat cushions help you swing your legs into the car with less twisting. Pedal extenders bring the gas and brake closer, easing pressure on hips and knees without forcing you too close to the dashboard. These modifications are affordable, easy to install, and often reduce fatigue even on short drives.

Simple stretches before driving also help. Try rolling your shoulders in slow circles five times each way, gently turning your head side to side, and flexing your wrists and fingers to keep them mobile. During longer drives, use red lights as reminders to shrug your shoulders or flex your hands. These small movements keep blood flowing and prevent joints from locking up.

If stiffness or pain is ongoing, physical or occupational therapy can provide tailored exercises—improving hip flexibility, strengthening grip, or easing back strain. Even at home, daily stretching routines or activities like walking, swimming, or senior fitness classes improve overall mobility, making driving easier and more comfortable.

If pain continues to interfere with your ability to drive safely, speak with your healthcare provider. New treatments, therapies, or adaptive devices may be available to support you.

Every driver deserves comfort and control. With the right modifications, simple routines, and professional support when needed, those familiar aches don't have to limit your independence on the road.

Cognitive Changes—Staying Focused and Avoiding Confusion

Mental sharpness can shift gradually with age. You may notice words slipping your mind or it taking longer to recall a familiar street name. Behind the wheel, these small lapses can feel larger—like when a left turn suddenly seems stressful in heavy traffic or when an unexpected detour slows your decision-making. Distractions such as a billboard or phone ring may also pull your attention away just long enough to miss something important.

These changes aren't a reason to doubt your ability—they're a reminder to adjust how you drive. Concentration deserves the same care as any other skill. Start by limiting distractions. Silence your phone, keep music low, and reduce anything that clouds your focus. Planning ahead also helps. Write down directions in large print or keep a simple note of your errands where it's easy to glance at but not in your way.

Forming habits that reinforce memory can make driving less stressful. Say your plan out loud before leaving: "Pharmacy, then the bank, then the grocery store." If remembering tasks feels harder than usual, shorten your list or simplify your trip.

Self-checks can be simple and even useful beyond driving. Try memorizing three or four errands before leaving and see if you recall them afterward without looking. Or keep a small notebook in your glove box to record moments when you felt confused by directions, missed a turn, or forgot where you parked. Over time, patterns may appear that are worth discussing with someone you trust.

If confusion becomes frequent—such as feeling lost on familiar roads or forgetting basic traffic rules—it's time to talk openly with your doctor. Memory specialists can determine whether the changes are normal aging or something that needs attention. Early evaluation often brings peace of mind and strategies to adapt, helping you stay independent longer.

Driving requires mental clarity, but with honest self-checks and a few simple adjustments, many seniors remain sharp and capable on the road. Staying safe means watching your focus as closely as you do the traffic—and being willing to seek support when needed.

6

Chapter 3: Planning for Safe and Stress-Free Trips

Choosing the Best Time to Travel—Avoiding Rush Hour and Night Driving

A trip across town can feel very different depending on when you go. Leaving at 2:00 pm might mean smooth sailing, while the same drive at 5:00 pm can turn into bumper-to-bumper frustration. Timing isn't just about convenience—it affects your safety and comfort. It's easier to arrive calm and confident when you avoid long waits, tense drivers, and harsh glare.

Rush hour—early mornings and late afternoons—brings more than delays. Accidents are more common in heavy traffic, where drivers weave, brake suddenly, and grow impatient. Even in smaller towns, school pick-up times, work shifts, or busy shopping centers create peak periods with added stress and unpredictability.

Driving after dark presents a different challenge. Reduced light strains your eyes, while glare from oncoming headlights—especially bright LEDs—can momentarily blind you. Street signs are harder to read, pedestrians blend into shadows, and distance is tougher to judge. These issues often intensify with age or corrective lenses, making night driving especially taxing.

The key is to know when and where conditions are easiest. Start by learning your community's traffic patterns. Apps like Google Maps show real-time and predicted congestion with clear, yellow, or red lines—helping you time your trip to avoid the worst of it. If you prefer low-tech methods, listen to local radio or chat with neighbors to learn when and where slowdowns happen. From there, block out your own "safe travel windows"—perhaps mid-morning or after the evening rush—when roads are calmer.

Night driving isn't always avoidable, but preparation makes a difference. Keep headlights clean, bright, and properly aimed; even a quick wipe can improve visibility. Ask your mechanic to check them during routine service. Whenever possible, schedule important errands during daylight or early evening, and keep late-night trips short and to well-lit routes. If you must drive in the dark, avoid staring at oncoming headlights; instead, focus on the right edge of your lane until they pass. Lower your dashboard lights to reduce glare without losing visibility.

Finally, consider creating a personal "safe driving schedule." Review your weekly errands and appointments, avoid high-risk times like rush hour or dusk, and shift activities into mid-morning or early afternoon when possible. Let friends or family know your preferred driving windows so they can help you stick to them.

Reflection: Creating Your Safe Driving Schedule

Take a piece of paper or your planner and note when traffic is lightest— maybe 9:30 am to 11:30 am, or 1:30 pm to 3:30 pm. Mark evenings, school pick-up times, or other periods when driving is tougher. Write down your appointments next to these safe windows. If something falls at a crowded or dark time—like a doctor's visit at sunset—see if you can reschedule. Keep this list somewhere visible, like near your phone or on the fridge, to check before heading out.

By making small changes in when you travel, you can enjoy calmer roads, fewer close calls, and a more relaxed arrival. You deserve trips that feel peaceful, not pressured—and choosing the right timing is one of the best ways to make that happen.

Mapping Out Easy-to-Navigate Routes

The routes you choose can shape how confident you feel behind the wheel. A simple, familiar road often makes the difference between a calm drive and a stressful one. Many seniors find main streets easier than shortcuts or backroads. Main roads usually have clearer signs, steadier traffic signals, and better lighting, while shortcuts can bring tricky merges, sharp turns, or confusing lane changes. Even if a shortcut looks faster on paper, the peace of mind from a straightforward route is often worth the extra few minutes.

One of the best tips is to reduce left turns across busy lanes. Judging the speed of oncoming traffic in multiple lanes can be stressful. Instead, choose routes with traffic lights or plan loops using mostly right turns. Some drivers even organize their errands to avoid left turns altogether, making the trip smoother and less nerve-racking.

Maps and technology can also help. Keep a current paper map in your glove box as a backup, ideally in large print so it's easy to read. Many drivers prefer navigation apps like Google Maps, which allow you to adjust your route. Under "Route Options," you can choose to avoid highways, tolls, or ferries—useful if you'd rather stick to main streets. Preview the route before leaving so you're familiar with the steps and any tricky intersections.

If you prefer printed directions, increase the font size before printing so each turn is clear and bold. Place the sheet within reach and trace the route with your finger before leaving to visualize each turn.

Preparation also helps when plans change. Missed turns or detours can rattle anyone, so it's smart to note a couple of alternate routes. Often, knowing which major cross streets run parallel is enough. Plan safe pull-over spots, like gas stations or large parking lots, where you can stop to reorient yourself.

Finally, remember that technology is a tool, not a rule. If your GPS gives confusing directions, don't feel pressured to follow them. Pull over safely, review your notes or map, and proceed at your own pace. You're the one in control.

Planning Your Route Worksheet

Here's a simple worksheet that many seniors find helpful before every drive. Fill it out at home before you leave:

1. My main route will be: _____

   _____

2. My backup route (if needed) will be: _____

   _____

3. Major cross streets or landmarks along my way: _____

   _____

4. Places I can safely pull over if needed: _____

   _____

5. Any left turns I can avoid? _____

   _____

6. Print directions ready? Y/N Map in car? Y/N

Keep this worksheet by your keys or phone as a visual reminder whenever you plan an outing. Writing things down helps cement the plan in your mind and gives you a sense of control over your trip.

Choosing easy-to-navigate routes is an act of self-care and wisdom—not a sign of weakness or fear. It means you value your comfort and safety above speed or shortcuts. With some planning, a good map, and backup ideas ready, every drive becomes less stressful and much more enjoyable.

Preparing for the Unexpected—Weather, Detours, and Traffic

No matter how carefully you plan, the road can surprise you. A sunny morning can turn stormy by afternoon, or a familiar street may be blocked with cones and detour signs. Even smooth trips can shift into brake lights and congestion without warning. These moments can rattle any driver, but with preparation and a flexible mindset, you can handle them safely.

Checking the weather before you leave is one of the smartest habits you can build. Rain, fog, ice, and wind can all make driving more demanding. Most smartphones have built-in weather apps, or you can use ones like Weather Channel or AccuWeather. Set the display to large text for easy reading. Check conditions for your starting point, destination, and return time. If storms are expected, consider delaying your trip or adjusting your plans. Your state's transportation website or hotline is another great tool—many post real-time updates on accidents, closures, and hazardous conditions. Bookmark the link or save the number so it's always close at hand.

Detours and construction zones are another common challenge. Bright orange signs can appear suddenly, redirecting you to unfamiliar roads. Most detour signs use arrows or phrases like "Road Closed" or "Follow Detour." If you're unsure, slow down and look for workers or flaggers who can guide you. Keep a small notepad in your glove box with a few alternate routes written down. Knowing parallel streets or cross-street connections ahead of time makes detours much less stressful.

If construction blocks your path or slows traffic, don't hesitate to pull into a safe spot—such as a shopping center lot or rest area—to regroup. Taking a few minutes to breathe, review your map, or check your app can make the rest of your drive smoother.

Traffic jams can also test your patience. Stop-and-go movement can trigger anxiety, but calming strategies help. Try breathing in through your nose for four counts, then exhaling slowly through your mouth for six. This slows your heart rate and keeps you steady. Playing soft, familiar music can also reduce stress and make the wait feel easier.

Sometimes plans simply need to change. A storm may roll in, a bridge might close, or you may realize your energy isn't what you expected. The key is adaptability. Adjusting your plan is not a setback—it's a smart way to stay safe and in control.

Checklist: What to Do If Plans Change

- Find a safe place to pull over—look for well-lit parking lots or rest areas.
- Take a few deep breaths; drink water if you have it.
- Check the weather app or state transportation website for updates.
- Review backup routes using your map or app.
- Call ahead if someone is expecting you—let them know about the delay.
- Reassess whether you want to continue or wait out conditions.
- If needed, ask for help—a family member or friend may be available to talk through options.

By building these habits into every trip, you'll find that even when surprises show up—a sudden downpour, confusing detour sign, or bumper-to-bumper jam—you're ready with practical steps. You don't have to race against the clock or white-knuckle through stress; instead, you move at your own pace, always with a backup plan in your back pocket. That's real peace of mind behind the wheel.

Packing for Comfort—What to Bring for Every Drive

Before setting off, think about comfort and safety, not just the destination. A little preparation can turn a stressful outing into a relaxed drive. The bag you bring—and how you organize your car—makes a big difference.

Start with the basics: carry a water bottle to stay hydrated and keep your energy steady. Healthy snacks like granola bars, almonds, or apple slices help prevent fatigue if a short trip turns into a long one. Sunglasses are essential for managing glare, and a sturdy sun visor adds extra protection. Always bring a fully charged cell phone with a charging cable for directions or emergencies.

If you have medical needs, preparation is about independence as much as comfort. Use a labeled pill organizer for medications so you don't miss doses if you're out longer than expected. Keep spare hearing aid batteries in a small pouch and carry an extra pair of glasses in case yours break or get misplaced.

Organization matters, too. A cluttered seat or floor creates distractions. Seatback organizers or console caddies help keep items within reach and in their own spots—snacks in one pocket, glasses in another, and medications zipped up securely. If you use a cane or walker, store it where it's stable and easy to grab, not rolling loose on the floor.

Consider creating a "go bag" that stays in your car at all times. A small tote can hold an emergency contact card, first-aid kit, blanket, and lightweight pillow for long waits or unexpected delays. Add personal essentials like tissues, sanitizer, or sunscreen. Tape a checklist inside the bag as a reminder: water, snacks, medications, batteries, glasses, phone, contacts, and blanket. Replace items right away if you use them so the bag stays ready.

Some people keep a second go bag at home for swapping seasonal items—gloves and hand warmers in winter, sunscreen and bug spray in summer. This makes it simple to stay prepared year-round.

Being prepared isn't about expecting problems; it's about making every outing more comfortable and secure. When everything you need is close at hand and neatly organized, you're free to focus on the road and enjoy the drive with confidence.

Using Checklists to Prepare for Every Trip

There's something comforting about knowing you've covered all your bases before leaving home. Over the years, I've found that having a checklist—written out, not just in my head—makes each trip feel less rushed and far more manageable. Checklists work a bit like a silent co-pilot, keeping your mind focused and reducing the worry that you might forget something important. They're especially handy when routines get interrupted, like on days when you're running late or feeling scattered. Many older adults tell me that anxiety about missing a step—like forgetting to buckle up or check the gas gauge—

fades away with a simple, clear list in hand. These lists don't just help with memory lapses; they also take pressure off your mind, freeing you up to concentrate on the road instead of nagging doubts about what you might have missed.

For those who appreciate a steady routine, a pre-drive checklist quickly becomes second nature. Before each outing, run through your own set of steps. Start by checking your fuel level. There's nothing worse than realizing you're running on empty halfway to your destination. Next, look over your tire pressure; properly inflated tires not only improve safety but make for a smoother ride. Adjust your mirrors and seat so everything feels comfortable and you have a clear view in every direction. I always remind myself to double-check that my registration and insurance cards are tucked in the glove box, and that my phone is charged and within easy reach (but not in my lap or hand while driving). Some folks like to write their checklist on a large-font card and tape it near the door or keep it in the visor—whatever makes it visible and easy to use.

Here's a sample "before you go" checklist you can print, copy, or personalize for your needs:

Before You Go Checklist

- Fuel tank at least half full
- Tire pressure looks good
- Mirrors clean and adjusted
- Seat in comfortable position
- Registration and insurance in car
- Phone charged and stored safely
- Glasses or hearing aids ready (if needed)
- Route reviewed and printed/loaded on GPS
- Comfort kit packed (snacks, water, meds)

Feel free to add or subtract from this list based on what fits you. Maybe you want to include checking your wallet for cash or making sure your garage door remote is working.

The return trip deserves just as much attention. After a busy outing, it's easy to forget that conditions may have changed since you first left home. Before heading back, pause for a moment and run through a quick mental or written "return" checklist. Make sure you remember your planned route home, and check if weather or traffic conditions have shifted—a quick look at your phone's weather app or listening to the car radio can provide updates. If you've bought groceries or run errands, secure bags and packages so they won't roll around or distract you as you drive. Double-check that your comfort kit is still stocked. If you ate your snack or finished your water on the way out, restock before leaving for home.

Sometimes it helps to ask for another set of eyes. Having a loved one or friend review your checklist can bring peace of mind—especially before longer trips or when trying new routines. Don't be shy about inviting someone to be your co-pilot for the day. They can help by reading directions aloud, reminding you of stops along the way, or simply checking that nothing was left behind at your last destination. If you're carrying medications, ask them to confirm you have enough for the entire excursion. I know some folks who make this a social habit—reviewing checklists together over coffee before leaving for an outing.

If you prefer independence but still want support, share your checklist with family ahead of time. Let them know what steps matter most to you, and invite their suggestions. Sometimes a fresh perspective highlights steps that could make things even smoother—like adding "check sunglasses" on sunny days or "bring extra batteries" if hearing aids are needed.

Checklists are much more than reminders written on paper—they're practical tools for living with confidence and reducing stress. They support good habits, prevent small problems from becoming big headaches, and help every drive start (and end) on the right foot.

Chapter 4: Staying Alert and Focused Behind the Wheel

The Power of Rest—Sleep, Breaks, and Fatigue Management

Think about the difference between a well-rested morning and one after a poor night's sleep. When you're rested, your mind feels sharp, your body alert, and decisions come easily. But when you're tired, reaction time slows, focus fades, and even simple choices feel harder. Now picture driving in that state. Fatigue isn't just uncomfortable—it's dangerous.

Older adults are especially sensitive to missed sleep, and research shows that getting less than seven hours a night increases the risk of mistakes behind the wheel. Drowsy driving causes thousands of accidents every year, and for drivers 65 and older, fatigue is a major factor in higher crash rates per mile compared with younger drivers. You don't have to fall asleep at the wheel to be at risk—zoning out, drifting from your lane, or missing a turn can all lead to serious consequences.

Recognizing the early signs of fatigue is one of your best defenses. Physical cues include frequent yawning, rubbing your eyes, heavy eyelids, or brief moments of blurred vision. Mentally, you may find yourself daydreaming, losing track of where you are, or making small mistakes like missing an exit. Irritability is another red flag—if every red light feels like a personal insult, fatigue may be the cause. More severe warning signs include nodding off, slumping in your seat, or blinking for longer than usual. These signals all point to one thing: it's time to rest before you continue driving.

Fatigue Warning Signs Checklist

- Frequent yawning or rubbing eyes
- Heavy or drooping eyelids
- Blurred vision or trouble focusing
- Daydreaming or wandering thoughts
- Missing exits or turns
- Feeling irritable or impatient
- Difficulty remembering the last few miles
- Head nodding or sudden jerks awake

If you notice even one or two of these signs before driving, it's best to postpone your trip. If they appear while on the road, pull over safely and rest.

Improving rest starts the night before. Keep a steady bedtime routine: dim the lights an hour before bed, avoid caffeine after lunch, and keep electronics out of the bedroom. Many people find that reading or listening to soft music helps them wind down. If pain or medication interrupts sleep, talk with your doctor. Aim for seven to eight hours of rest each night to support focus and energy.

On the road, breaks are more than pit stops—they're essential for alertness. Follow the "two-hour rule": stop at least every two hours for a fifteen-minute break. Even on short trips, stretch your legs if you feel stiff or groggy. Walk around the car, loosen your arms and neck, or do a few gentle stretches before getting back in. If drowsiness hits mid-trip, find a safe place to park and take a nap. Even twenty minutes can restore clarity far better than pushing through fatigue.

Schedule breaks into your outings, whether at a park bench, coffee shop, or simply a rest area. Use your phone's alarm feature to remind you every 90 minutes to check in with yourself.

A personal rest routine makes these habits automatic. Before each drive, ask yourself: *Did I sleep well last night? Am I fully alert?* If not, reschedule non-essential trips or ask for help. For longer drives, plan your rest stops in advance and stick to them.

Some seniors keep a notepad in the glove box to track sleep quality, energy level, and moments of fatigue. Over time, these notes reveal patterns that help with safer trip planning.

You deserve drives that feel steady and secure, not clouded by drowsiness or distraction. By making rest and breaks part of your routine, you protect yourself and everyone who shares the road.

Creating a Distraction-Free Driving Environment

Cars fill up with distractions more easily than we realize. Passengers may chat or ask questions, the dashboard glows with lights and buttons, and loose items roll noisily across the floor. A phone chimes with text alerts, the radio jumps into a commercial, or a pair of glasses slips from the dash at just the wrong moment. Even small interruptions can chip away at focus and increase the chance of mistakes. For many older adults, modern dashboards with tiny screens or multiple touch controls can feel especially overwhelming.

The best defense is to prepare before starting the car. Silence your phone or switch it to "Do Not Disturb" mode, and set up navigation in advance with the phone secured in a mount—not on the seat or in your lap. Clear away bags, bottles, coins, or anything that could slide or rattle if you stop suddenly. Use a glove box, console, or seat organizer to keep items out of sight and within reach. Store glasses in a sturdy case nearby, and if you wear hearing aids, make sure they're adjusted comfortably with spare batteries packed.

Decluttering the dashboard also makes a difference. Remove old papers, cords, or anything blocking displays. Adjust climate controls, music, or audiobooks before you pull out, and set the volume so it won't need changing mid-trip. Choosing playlists or stations in advance helps avoid fiddling while driving.

Passengers can be both enjoyable and distracting. Grandchildren may pepper you with questions, while friends might talk nonstop or offer unsolicited advice. It's perfectly reasonable to set boundaries. Try: "I need to focus on the road, so let's catch up when we arrive," or, "If I ask for help with directions, please read them slowly out loud." If a co-pilot wants to help, give them specific tasks—like handling the phone, adjusting the GPS, or watching for turns—so their help reduces stress rather than adding to it.

These boundaries don't have to feel awkward. A simple request such as, "When I'm driving, it helps if you watch for my next turn," often makes passengers eager to support your safety.

Finally, consider doing a quick "distraction audit" before every drive. Ask yourself: What usually pulls my focus away from the road? Is it reaching for sunglasses, adjusting a seatbelt, or digging into the backseat for something forgotten? By anticipating these distractions and solving them before you leave, you set yourself up for a calmer, safer trip.

Distraction Audit Checklist

- Is my phone turned off or set to "Do Not Disturb"?
- Have I secured all loose items in bins or compartments?
- Are my glasses and hearing aids within easy reach and functioning?
- Is my dashboard clear of unnecessary items?
- Have I set my music/radio before starting the drive?
- Did I adjust my seatbelt and mirrors before pulling out?
- Have I explained my preferences to passengers about conversation and assistance?
- Is my navigation system programmed and mounted securely?

Take a moment to review this list each time you prepare for an outing. Tweaking your routine may feel odd at first but will soon become second nature. The less clutter and chaos in your car—both physical and mental—the more peace of mind you'll feel on every drive.

Small details make a big difference in keeping focus where it belongs: on the road ahead. When distractions are managed ahead of time, your mind is clearer, reaction times sharper, and driving feels more relaxed—not just for you but everyone sharing the ride.

Mindful Driving—Techniques for Staying Present

Mindful driving means giving your full attention to the road, your hands on the wheel, and the world around you. It's not about emptying your mind—it's about noticing what's happening in the present moment. For seniors, this focus can reduce mistakes and calm anxiety, making driving feel steadier and more enjoyable. When you're present, you're less likely to miss a sign, overlook a pedestrian, or let worry take over.

You can build this habit with simple, everyday practices. Before turning the key, take a slow breath and notice three things outside—maybe a child biking past, the sound of birds, or the color of a neighbor's mailbox. This quick check-in roots you in the moment and sharpens your senses for the drive ahead. At stoplights, use the pause to reset: place both feet on the floor, sit tall, and inhale slowly through your nose. Exhale through your mouth and let your shoulders drop. These small resets help release tension and bring your focus back.

If worries creep in mid-drive—like thoughts about an appointment or parking—try grounding exercises. Grip the steering wheel and notice its texture and temperature. Name what you feel: smooth, soft, cool, or warm. This physical focus pulls your attention back to the present. Another option is to engage your senses in pairs. Quietly name two things you see—a red car, a row of trees—and two things you hear—the hum of the engine, distant voices. Cycling through sight and sound can quickly clear away distractions.

If persistent worries pop up, acknowledge them without judgment— "There's that thought again"—and gently redirect your attention. Some people find it grounding to narrate aloud: "I'm driving on Main Street. The light ahead is red. I'm safe." This running commentary keeps your focus on what's real, not on anxious thoughts.

Real experiences show how effective this can be. Ruth, who felt anxious at a busy intersection near her home, began taking three slow breaths before her turn while naming one thing she saw in each direction—left, center, right. She found it eased her nerves and made her more alert to traffic and pedestrians. George, a retired postal worker, was skeptical but tried deep breathing at stoplights. He noticed his hands unclenched from the wheel and, over time, his heart raced less in traffic and he made fewer mistakes merging or turning.

If you'd like, keep a small notebook in your car to jot down one thing you noticed on each trip—a cheerful crossing guard, blooming flowers, or the smell of fresh-cut grass. These simple notes remind you that mindful moments are always available.

Mindfulness builds gradually, like any good habit. You don't need special training—just a willingness to pause, notice, and return your attention when distractions pull you away. Each mindful moment adds up to calmer, safer miles on the road, helping you stay alert in both body and spirit.

Scanning for Hazards—Mastering the Mirror Check

Staying alert behind the wheel isn't just about keeping your eyes open—it's about knowing where to look, how often, and what to expect. As reaction times slow and peripheral vision changes with age, deliberate scanning becomes one of the most important habits you can build. This isn't about being nervous— it's about turning observation into a routine that keeps you prepared every time you drive.

Start with your mirrors. Don't limit them to lane changes or backing up— make it a habit to check all three mirrors often. Think of it as a rhythm: eyes forward, rearview, left mirror, right mirror, back to the road ahead. This sweep helps you spot motorcycles, cyclists, or fast-moving vehicles before they're a problem. The more consistently you practice, the more automatic it becomes.

Begin each trip by checking mirror placement. The rearview should frame the entire rear window, while each side mirror should show just the edge of your car with the rest covering the adjacent lanes. Once driving, maintain that steady rhythm of glances. If needed, count "one Mississippi" as a timer or ask a friend to ride along and remind you until it feels natural.

Intersections deserve extra care. Before moving through any crossing—busy or quiet—use a "left-center-right" scan. Check left first for approaching cars, then center for cross traffic or red-light runners, and finally right for pedestrians or late arrivals. Take your time; an extra heartbeat before pulling forward can prevent a close call.

Road edges also matter. Seniors sometimes miss quick movement in their peripheral vision, so sweep curbs, sidewalks, and driveways as you drive. Watch for cyclists behind parked cars, children chasing balls, or pets darting into the street. Hazards often appear just outside the main roadway.

You can practice these habits in a safe space. While parked, rehearse your mirror sweep: rearview, left, right, back ahead. To sharpen awareness, ask a co-pilot to move around your car while you track them in your mirrors, calling out when you see them. Another drill is to stay seated while a partner walks at different distances around the vehicle. Signal "now" when they enter your view—this builds confidence that your checks are catching what they should.

Consistency is the goal. By turning mirror sweeps and hazard scans into muscle memory, you'll drive more confidently and with less stress. These simple, deliberate habits are among the strongest defenses you have against the unexpected and help ensure every trip is a safe one.

Mirror Check Routine Checklist

Use this as a quick reminder before and during each drive.

Before Driving

- Adjust mirrors so the rearview shows the entire back window.
- Set side mirrors so only the edge of your car is visible, with the rest showing the lane beside you.

While Driving

- Sweep mirrors often: rearview → left mirror → right mirror → eyes back to the road ahead.
- Count "one Mississippi" to keep intervals steady until it feels natural.

At Intersections

- Use the "left-center-right" scan before moving forward.
- Look for cars, pedestrians, and cyclists coming from all directions.

Along Road Edges

- Scan sidewalks, curbs, and driveways for movement—children, pets, or cyclists may enter suddenly.

Practice Drills

- Rehearse mirror sweeps while parked.
- Ask a co-pilot to walk around the car and track them using only mirrors.

Recognizing and Responding to Drowsiness or Overwhelm

Every driver, no matter how experienced, is vulnerable to spells of drowsiness or moments when the mind feels flooded. You might notice yourself missing road signs you usually catch without a second thought, blinking more than usual, or watching your thoughts meander far from the task at hand. Sometimes, you realize you've just driven several blocks but can't quite remember passing that last intersection. Other warning signs surface in your body: a heavy sensation behind your eyes, hands gripping the steering wheel a bit too tightly, or that odd feeling of losing track of where you are in a familiar neighborhood. These are real signals that your mind is checking out, even if just for a second. Wandering thoughts can be sneaky, pulling you away from what matters most—your safety and that of others. Recognizing these moments early makes all the difference.

Drowsiness and Cognitive Overload Warning Signs Checklist

- Missing or misreading road signs
- Frequent blinking or rubbing your eyes
- Daydreaming or drifting thoughts
- Feeling lost on familiar routes
- Forgetting recent traffic lights or turns
- Struggling to recall your destination
- Feeling overwhelmed by traffic or directions
- Reacting slowly to sudden traffic changes

If you notice one or more of these while driving, take action immediately. Don't push through—your safety comes first. Find a safe place to pull over, such as a parking lot, rest area, or wide shoulder on a quiet street. Shift into park, turn off the engine if you plan to stay a while, and give yourself permission to regroup. Fresh air, a splash of water, or simply closing your eyes for a few minutes can make a big difference.

Overwhelm can strike in heavy traffic, on detours, or when surrounded by impatient drivers. In those moments, use grounding techniques. Try slow, steady breathing: inhale for four counts, hold for two, then exhale for six. This relaxes your body and sharpens focus. Positive self-talk helps too: "I've handled tough drives before," or, "I can pause and figure this out." These phrases quiet stress and bring attention back to what matters most.

If the fog doesn't lift—say you're stuck in gridlock or still feel off—it's wise to end your drive early. Keeping a backup plan ready is part of safe, independent driving. Rideshare apps like Uber or Lyft, or a trusted friend or neighbor's phone number, give you options when continuing isn't safe. If you're new to rideshare apps, ask a family member or neighbor to walk you through setup, and try a short practice ride so you know how it works when you need it.

Some days, shifting from driver to passenger is the smartest choice you can make. Checking in with yourself throughout each drive ensures you stay in control—not only of your car, but of your long-term independence. Each time you respond wisely to warning signs, you're choosing safety over stubbornness and protecting your freedom for the miles ahead.

Alertness is never automatic—it's built through awareness and self-honesty on every trip. By paying attention to how you feel, you keep yourself safe today and lay the groundwork for confidence tomorrow. Up next, we'll explore strategies for handling life's trickier driving situations—intersections, freeways, and unpredictable weather—so you're prepared for whatever the road brings.

8

Chapter 5: Handling Challenging Situations on the Road

Navigating Intersections with Confidence

Intersections come in many forms—four-way stops, T-intersections, round-abouts, and unprotected left turns. Each brings unique challenges, and it's natural to feel more cautious with age as vision, reaction time, and processing speed gradually change. The key to confidence is having a consistent, deliberate approach.

At a four-way stop, cars should proceed in the order they arrive, but confusion arises when someone rolls through or waves you ahead out of turn. T-intersections can also trip drivers up if right of way isn't clear, remember the through street has the right of way. Roundabouts may seem intimidating, but the rules are simple: slow down, yield to cars already inside the circle, and wait for a safe gap before entering. Stay in your lane, signal right before your exit, and check for pedestrians. If you miss your exit, circle around again—it's safer than rushing.

Unprotected left turns often cause the most stress. Judging speed and distance of oncoming traffic is harder than it seems, especially when cars move quickly or are hidden by curves. The best approach is patience: ease forward only when you see a safe, comfortable gap. Never let honking or impatience push you into a risky decision.

Hidden or confusing signs add another layer of challenge. In unfamiliar areas, look well ahead for painted lane arrows, traffic patterns, or stopped cars that may reveal what's coming. Be alert for temporary detour signs or faded pavement markings that could affect your next move.

A steady scanning habit keeps you safe. As you near the intersection, slow down and do a "left-center-right" check: left for oncoming cars or cyclists, center for cross-traffic or pedestrians, and right for late arrivals or red-light runners. If you're first when a light turns green, pause just a moment before proceeding—this extra heartbeat can prevent a collision with someone running a red light.

Signal at least 100 feet before your turn, keep both hands on the wheel, and avoid distractions as you move through. Safety is about clarity, not speed. As one friend of mine put it after freezing at a suburban intersection, "It wasn't that I didn't know how to turn—I just needed a little more certainty." That moment of hesitation isn't weakness; it's wisdom.

Above all, never let the pressure of others override your judgment. If you're uncertain, remember the simple rule: *When in doubt, wait it out.* Lights will cycle again, gaps will appear, and it's always better to arrive late than to risk your safety.

Intersection Confidence Checklist

- Slow down well before the intersection.
- Do a left-center-right check.
- Signal early.
- Verify the path is clear—don't rush.
- Make eye contact with other drivers if possible.
- For left turns: proceed only if the gap feels comfortable.
- If uncertain, wait for the next light or a safer gap.

Keep this checklist handy in your car for quick reference before approaching challenging intersections.

Mistakes like rushing a yellow light or stalling in an intersection usually happen from feeling hurried or doubting your judgment. Trust yourself. If you find hesitation is frequent, consider a refresher course or practice with a trusted co-driver. Even discussing your worries with family can help restore confidence.

Intersections don't have to feel overwhelming. With a solid routine and patience, they become manageable and safe parts of your trip.

Merging and Changing Lanes on Busy Turnpikes

Merging onto a busy turnpike or shifting lanes in fast-moving traffic can feel intimidating, but with the right routine, these maneuvers become smoother and safer. The key is preparation and timing.

When approaching an on-ramp, begin watching the flow of traffic well before the merge point. Notice vehicle speed and the space between cars. Use the acceleration lane as your buffer zone to gradually match the pace of traffic. Too slow, and you'll force others to brake; too fast, and you may miss your gap. Keep a steady foot on the gas as you near the merge, so other drivers can anticipate your move. If traffic is heavy and openings are tight, stay calm and look for your opportunity. Lingering at the end of the ramp is riskier than blending in smoothly when space allows.

For both merging and lane changes, rely on a steady routine: *mirror, signal, blind spot, go.* First, check your mirrors to see who's around you. Next, signal early—giving others time to adjust. Then, quickly glance over your shoulder to cover blind spots. Once the way is clear, ease into the lane smoothly. Avoid jerking the wheel or hesitating mid-move, as both can unsettle surrounding traffic.

If anxiety makes merging stressful, practice in a no-pressure setting. An empty parking lot works well: set up cones or markers, then rehearse signaling, checking mirrors, and steering into "lanes." These dry runs build confidence and muscle memory without the stress of real traffic.

There will be times when merging or changing lanes simply isn't safe—

such as in heavy rain, poor visibility, or dense traffic that leaves no room to maneuver. In those situations, it's wise to wait, adjust your route, or even exit early and re-enter where traffic is lighter. Skipping a risky lane change or delaying a merge isn't a sign of weakness—it's good judgment.

With steady habits and patience, merging and lane changes become less about tension and more about confidence. Every smooth, deliberate move reinforces your control and helps keep both you and those around you safer on the road.

Checklist for Safe Merging Conditions

- Am I approaching at a speed similar to traffic?
- Are there clear gaps large enough for my car?
- Have I checked all mirrors and my blind spot?
- Did I signal well in advance?
- Does the maneuver feel controlled—not rushed or forced?
- Would waiting or taking an alternate exit reduce risk?

If you answer "no" to any of these, consider holding off. Sometimes easing off at an earlier exit to avoid last-second merges or lane changes can save you a great deal of stress.

The road isn't a racetrack—your safety is always more important than reaching your destination a few minutes sooner. Small adjustments in timing and routine can make busy highways less intimidating and restore a feeling of control behind the wheel.

Freeway Driving—Staying Safe at Higher Speeds

Freeways offer both freedom and challenges. With higher speeds and fewer cross-streets or pedestrians, the ride can feel smooth and steady—but every mistake carries greater weight when traffic is moving at 65 miles per hour or more. Lane changes happen faster, reaction times matter more, and the flow can feel intimidating. Still, with steady habits, freeway driving can be safe and manageable.

Lane discipline is key. The right and middle lanes usually provide the calmest experience, while the far left lane is best reserved for passing or drivers comfortable at higher speeds. Keep a safe cushion between you and the car ahead by using the "three-second rule." Choose a landmark—like a sign or overpass. When the vehicle in front passes it, count: *one thousand one, one thousand two, one thousand three.* Your bumper shouldn't reach that spot before you finish counting. In rain or heavy traffic, stretch it to four or five seconds. Cruise control can help prevent drifting over the limit, but avoid it in heavy rain or on curvy stretches.

Exits can approach quickly, so plan ahead. Watch for green guide signs a mile in advance and begin moving right early to avoid last-second lane changes. Signal at least 300 feet before the ramp, then use the deceleration lane to ease off the gas and brake gradually. Sudden stops create risks for you and those behind you.

Here is a Safe Exit Checklist

- Know your exit number before you leave.
- Watch for signs at least one mile ahead.
- Signal early and merge right with plenty of space.
- Enter the deceleration lane smoothly.
- Ease off the gas, brake gently, and prepare for merging traffic or ramp slowdowns.

Aggressive drivers are part of the freeway landscape. Tailgaters may flash lights or weave impatiently. Remember: their rush is not your emergency. If someone follows too closely, signal and shift right when safe to let them pass. Avoid eye contact or gestures—responding only escalates tension. Keep your focus on your own lane, hands steady on the wheel, and speed consistent. If you feel unsafe, take the next exit or pull into a rest area to regroup. Lock your doors, keep windows up, and practice calming self-talk: *"I'm in control of my car. Their behavior doesn't control me."*

Freeway driving isn't about speed—it's about steadiness. Each trip builds confidence when you read the road ahead, give yourself space, and choose calm responses over confrontation. By sticking to safe habits, you'll find the freeway can feel less like a hurdle and more like a straightforward path to your destination.

Safe Driving in Rain, Fog, and Snow

Bad weather can turn a routine drive into a real challenge. Rain, fog, and snow each create unique risks, and for seniors—whose vision or reflexes may not be as sharp—these conditions deserve extra care.

Rain reduces visibility and makes the road slick, increasing stopping distance. Before you head out, check your tires with the penny test: if you can see the top of Lincoln's head, it's time for new ones. Inspect your wiper blades for cracks or streaking and top off windshield fluid. Keep headlights and taillights clean so you're visible to others. When driving, ease up on the gas and brake earlier than usual. Double your following distance and avoid cruise control on wet pavement. If your car begins to hydroplane, take your foot off the gas and steer steadily—don't slam the brakes.

Fog brings its own hazards by hiding signs, traffic lights, and even nearby cars. Use low beams—high beams only reflect off the mist and reduce visibility. If equipped, turn on fog lights for extra help, but don't rely on them alone. Slow down to a pace that matches what you can see. Open your window slightly to listen for traffic you may not spot. If lane lines disappear, use the right-hand markers or road edge as your guide.

Snow and ice can be the toughest conditions. Clear every window, mirror, and headlight before leaving—not just a small patch of windshield. Brush off the roof and hood so snow doesn't blow onto your view or another driver's. Slow down well before stop signs and intersections; even anti-lock brakes can't prevent sliding on ice. Brake gently, and if your car doesn't have ABS, pump the brakes lightly. If you skid, steer in the direction you want the front of your car to go and avoid sudden movements.

Sometimes conditions worsen after you've started. If rain becomes too heavy, snow falls faster than your wipers can handle, or fog reduces visibility to just a few car lengths, find a safe place to pull over. Use hazard lights, but choose a safe spot—a parking lot, rest stop, or wide shoulder away from curves and hills. When in doubt, wait it out. Stopping for coffee while a storm passes is far better than risking a drive you can't see through.

Always give yourself permission to change plans in bad weather. Your wellbeing comes first, not the schedule. Keeping a small emergency kit in your trunk—a blanket, flashlight, and water—adds peace of mind if you're delayed. In tough conditions, patience, preparation, and flexibility are your best tools for staying safe.

Bad Weather Safety Checklist

Rain

- Check tire tread with the penny test
- Inspect wipers and top off windshield fluid
- Clean headlights and taillights
- Double following distance
- Never use cruise control on wet roads
- If hydroplaning: ease off gas, steer steadily, don't brake hard

Fog

- Use low beams (never high beams)
- Turn on fog lights if available
- Slow to a pace that matches visibility
- Crack window to listen for traffic
- Follow right-hand markers or road edge as a guide

Snow & Ice

- Clear all windows, mirrors, headlights, roof, and hood
- Slow early for stops and intersections
- Brake gently (pump brakes if no ABS)
- Steer in the direction you want the front of your car to go

· Avoid sudden braking or sharp steering

General Tips

· Pull over safely if visibility drops too low
· Use hazard lights when stopped in poor conditions
· Keep an emergency kit: blanket, flashlight, water, and phone
· When in doubt, wait it out—your safety comes first

Parking Lots and Tight Spaces—Reducing Stress and Risk

Parking lots often feel more stressful than regular roads. Cars move unpredictably, pedestrians appear suddenly, and tall vehicles block visibility. Tight spaces also demand neck and shoulder flexibility, which can be tougher with age. Even backing out can feel like a challenge when mobility is limited.

The best way to reduce stress is to build a clear routine. Drive slowly and stay alert for movement—backup lights, feet under cars, or stray carts. Don't rush into the first spot you see. Instead, choose one with more room, even if it means walking farther. Pull-through spaces are ideal since they eliminate the need to reverse.

Whenever possible, back into a spot or drive through a spot to be able to exit going forward rather than reversing. If that was not an option and you need to back out, move slowly and follow a routine: check mirrors, glance at your backup camera if available, then turn to look over your shoulder. If twisting is difficult, rest your right hand on the passenger seat to help pivot your torso. If pedestrians appear, stop completely—never try to inch past. If you're unsure of what's behind you, ask a passenger to guide you from outside the car.

Lighting matters too. At night, choose well-lit areas that make both driving and walking safer. Parking farther from the entrance often means wider spaces and less distraction, which usually makes the entire outing easier.

If anxiety sets in, pause before maneuvering. Take a deep breath and remind yourself there's no rush. If the spot feels too tight, circle the lot again—choosing comfort over convenience is always the smarter option. Practice can also help: try parking drills in an empty lot during quiet hours to build confidence with reversing and turning.

Asking for help is never a weakness. A friend or family member signaling you in or out can save you stress and prevent accidents. Over time, these routines and tools will help transform parking from a nerve-wracking task into a manageable one.

Remember: the safest spot is the one that makes you feel most in control. Choose space, light, and calm over proximity, and every trip will start and end with less stress.

9

Chapter 6: Recognizing When Your Driving Needs to Change

Signs It Might Be Time to Reevaluate Your Driving

Picture a routine trip to the post office. You know the way by heart, yet you pause, suddenly uncertain. Or maybe you spot a new scratch on your car and can't remember how it happened. Small moments like these may seem harmless, but when they start adding up, they can be early warning signs that your driving is changing.

Subtle red flags often include more close calls, unexplained dents, or feeling lost on familiar routes. If you find yourself relying heavily on GPS, feeling anxious at intersections, or hesitating in traffic, your reaction time and confidence may not be what they once were.

Equally important are how you feel before and during drives. Sweaty palms, a racing heart, or constant "what if" worries can be just as significant as physical errors. Avoiding night driving or busy roads may reduce stress for now, but it also points to growing concerns.

Family and friends may notice changes before you do, such as missed stop signs, bumping curbs, or reacting too slowly to hazards. One mistake isn't unusual, but repeated incidents tell a clearer story. Recognizing these patterns isn't weakness—it's responsibility. Early adjustments—like avoiding high-stress times, updating your glasses prescription, or reviewing safe routes—can preserve independence and prevent accidents.

Reflection Exercise: Spotting Your Own Patterns

Take a moment to record recent uneasy driving experiences—missed turns, near misses, confusion at a light, new scrapes, or anxiety before or during a drive. Jot down what happened and how you felt—without judgment. If any experiences have repeated in the last month or two, circle them. Look for patterns; this isn't about blame, it's about honest self-awareness.

Noticing change is powerful; it shows you care about your safety and others'. Trust your instincts if something regularly feels off—they've guided you before. Recognizing change doesn't mean giving up, but rather choosing the safest, most dignified way forward.

Using Self-Assessment Checklists for Honest Reflection

Writing things down turns vague impressions into clear information. A self-assessment checklist helps you track how driving feels now and highlights areas where you may need adjustments.

Self-Assessment Driving Checklist

Rate each question:

0 – Never   1 – Rarely   2 – Sometimes   3 – Often   4 – Nearly every time

1. How comfortable do I feel driving at night or in bad weather?
2. Do I avoid highways, roundabouts, or busy intersections?
3. Can I handle detours and construction calmly?
4. Do I get lost even on familiar routes?
5. Am I able to tune out distractions from passengers, radio, or my phone?
6. How quickly do I respond to sudden stops or changes in traffic?
7. If someone cuts me off, do I stay composed or stay frustrated?
8. Do I often feel drained or anxious after driving?
9. Have I had near-misses, scrapes, or parking trouble recently?
10. Do I need frequent help finding my way on familiar routes?

Scoring:

- 0–10: No major concerns; keep monitoring.
- 11–20: Some "yellow flags"; consider small adjustments.
- 21+: "Red flags"; time for a deeper conversation with a doctor or trusted family member.

Repeat the checklist every six months, just like a regular health checkup. Keep your results in a notebook or folder to see if patterns develop over time. If certain questions keep landing in the "often" or "nearly every time" column, take note—it's valuable information.

Bring your checklist to your doctor's visit or share it with someone you trust. Their perspective can add context, since others may notice things you miss. If several red flags appear, talk through options together before problems grow.

This reflection takes courage, but it's a powerful way to protect both your safety and independence. Writing things down keeps you honest with yourself and creates opportunities for helpful conversations. Even if everything looks fine today, repeating the process regularly ensures that you'll spot changes early—and adapt while you're still in control.

Listening to Feedback from Family and Friends

Hearing comments about your driving from loved ones can sting, especially if you feel defensive. You may have decades of safe driving behind you, but those closest to you often notice subtle changes before you do. As passengers or fellow drivers, they may see hesitation at intersections or a missed stop sign—things you might brush off. Their perspective usually comes from care, not criticism. They want to keep you safe, not take away your independence.

Gradual changes are easy to miss when you're behind the wheel every day. Family may remember how confidently you once handled traffic and notice when you avoid certain roads or seem tense. Their questions—"Are you sure about driving at night?"—may feel uncomfortable, but they come from concern and love.

The key is responding calmly. Instead of dismissing concerns, acknowledge their effort: "Thank you for telling me. Can you share an example?" or

"I appreciate your honesty. Let's figure out a solution together." These responses encourage constructive feedback and reduce tension. You can also take the lead by asking: "Do you feel comfortable when I'm driving?" or "Have you noticed any changes?" This shows you value their perspective and makes the conversation less confrontational.

If you sense hesitation, reassure them: "I'd rather hear your thoughts now than risk an accident later." Inviting openness makes discussions more collaborative. Loved ones may suggest solutions like sharing driving duties or helping with errands. Instead of seeing these as a loss of independence, try to view them as support—mutual care that helps everyone.

When emotions run high, remind yourself and others that compromise is not defeat. Phrases like, "We all want what's best for each other," or, "Listening helps us stay independent longer," keep discussions respectful. If your family tends to be blunt, ask for clear ground rules: specific examples instead of vague comments, and discussions focused on solutions, not criticism.

Clarify what kind of feedback works best for you. Some prefer quick notes after a drive, while others prefer calm conversations later. If feedback feels overwhelming, it's okay to say, "I need time to think—let's talk tomorrow."

You may not agree with every suggestion, but seeing feedback as useful information—not a personal attack—protects your safety and dignity. Openness strengthens relationships, and involving loved ones in the process helps balance independence with necessary support. Honest conversations now mean more years of safe, confident driving together.

Medical Checkups and What to Ask Your Doctor

Annual checkups usually focus on flu shots, blood work, or aches and pains, but they're also a key opportunity to discuss how your health affects your driving. Regular conversations with your doctor can help protect both your safety and your independence on the road. Don't wait for your provider to bring it up—taking the lead ensures that important issues aren't overlooked.

Start with medications. Ask, *"Are any of my prescriptions likely to impact driving?"* Pain relievers, sleep aids, or blood pressure pills can sometimes cause drowsiness or slow reactions, especially when combined with other medicines. Bring an up-to-date list of everything you take, including over-the-counter items and supplements.

Check vision and hearing. Even small changes can blur road signs or make headlights more glaring. Ask, *"How often should I have my vision checked?"* or mention halos, glare, or trouble reading signs at night. For hearing, consider questions like, *"Do I need a referral for testing?"* or *"Are my hearing aids adjusted well enough to pick up traffic sounds?"*

Talk about cognition. Memory lapses, slower reactions, or trouble following directions can impact driving safety. A good question is, *"Are there changes in my thinking or memory that could affect my driving?"* Doctors can use simple screenings or refer you to specialists if needed.

Know when health changes should prompt review. Ask, *"What changes in my health should make me reconsider driving?"* Conditions such as stroke, diabetes, major medication changes, or hospital stays are all reasons to check your abilities.

Keep a driving health record. A simple notebook or folder works well. Record each visit with:

- Date and doctor's name
- Medication changes or warnings
- Vision and hearing test results
- Recommendations or next steps
- Follow-up appointment date

Bring this record to every visit, and ask specialists like eye doctors or neurologists to add notes relevant to driving.

Regular conversations about health and driving build confidence and reduce surprises. By raising the topic yourself and keeping clear records, you create a safety net of support from your doctor, family, and care team. Small steps like these help you stay independent, safe, and in control behind the wheel.

Understanding Road Tests and License Renewal After 65

The rules around keeping your driver's license change as you get older, and sometimes it feels like the goalposts move without warning. Most states require seniors to renew their licenses more often than younger adults. This might mean going in every two or four years instead of the longer stretches you may remember from your fifties. You might also find that mail-in or online renewals are no longer an option after a certain age, with in-person visits becoming the new standard. Some places add extra steps, like vision screenings or even written and road tests, especially after 70 or 75. In a few states, you'll be asked for a doctor's note or medical certification—proof that your eyesight, hearing, and general health are up to the demands of driving. For example, California requires in-person renewal and a vision test at age 70, while Illinois moves to annual renewals after 87, each time with a vision check. Alaska, Florida, and many others have their own timelines and rules for older drivers, so it pays to check your state's DMV website or ask for help reviewing the latest requirements.

The idea of taking a road test again after decades can be stressful. But with a little preparation, you can walk in feeling ready. Start with the basics: get a copy of your state's driver handbook—free from the DMV or online—and go through the sections covering safe driving habits. Practice reading road signs and reviewing right-of-way rules. These are often heavily tested. Many DMVs offer practice tests online that mimic the real thing; try a few until you feel comfortable. For the driving portion, focus on maneuvers that come up most often: follow speed limits, make safe lane changes, understand the right of way, merge safely onto the freeway. If it's been a while since your last test, don't be shy about taking a refresher course designed for older adults; these classes give you practical tips and boost your confidence.

Medical paperwork sometimes becomes part of the renewal process. You may need to bring a signed form from your doctor confirming your ability to drive safely—this could include results from vision and hearing tests, notes on medication side effects, or details about any long-term conditions like diabetes or arthritis. If your provider isn't sure what to write, offer a simple template: "I have examined [Your Name], who is under my care for [condition]. In my clinical opinion, [he/she/they] is able to operate a motor vehicle safely at this time." Some DMVs provide their own forms; print one out before your appointment so you're not caught off guard.

It's easy to see these extra steps as hurdles or even as punishment for getting older, but they are meant to keep both you and everyone around you safe on the road—not as a way to single out seniors unfairly. Passing these checks means you're still fit to drive, and catching issues early gives you a chance to adapt before problems grow. It also helps family members feel reassured about your safety. If you're worried about passing, know that there are many resources out there: AARP and AAA both offer online and classroom refresher courses specifically for seniors, and many community centers run group practice sessions before big renewal deadlines.

If you feel nervous about the whole process, remember that good preparation is the antidote to anxiety. Give yourself plenty of time before your license expires—don't leave the renewal until the last minute when nerves might get in the way. Bring your glasses or hearing aids if you use them; let the examiner know if you need extra time or have any mobility limitations. If you don't pass on your first try, it's normal—and it doesn't automatically mean you have to give up driving forever. Ask for feedback on what went wrong and focus on those skills before trying again.

Finishing up this chapter, it's clear that staying on the road after 65 means facing new rules and sometimes new challenges—but also brings fresh opportunities to grow and adapt. The process is not meant to take away your independence but to give you confidence in your abilities and peace of mind for every mile ahead. As we look forward to the next section, we'll explore how you can adjust driving habits and routines to fit this new stage, making each trip safe and rewarding.

10

Chapter 7: Preventing Conflict and Navigating Difficult Conversations

How to Talk About Driving with Loved Ones

Conversations about driving can be difficult, but starting them yourself shows strength and responsibility. Sitting down with family to discuss your driving habits, changes you've noticed, or concerns you may have is not about giving up independence—it's about protecting it. By opening the conversation, you show that you value both your safety and the well-being of those you love.

Before you bring it up, take a moment to check in with yourself. Are you nervous about how they might respond? Do you fear being misunderstood? Acknowledging those feelings helps you stay calm and clear when you speak. Remind yourself that this isn't a one-time decision—it's an ongoing conversation about how to keep you safe and confident on the road.

Choose the right time. Don't try to talk in a rush or when everyone's distracted. Instead, invite your family to sit down in a quiet, private space. You might say, *"There's something important I'd like to talk about. Can we sit together for a bit?"* Creating a calm setting shows that you're serious but also respectful.

When you begin, frame the conversation around your own experience. For example:

- *"Lately I've noticed driving at night feels harder for me—have you noticed that too?"*
- *"Sometimes I feel more stressed in busy intersections, and I'd like to talk about ways we can handle that together."*
- *"Driving has always been important to me, but I want to be realistic about how things are changing."*

These kinds of statements open the door without putting anyone on the defensive. They also make it clear that you're reflecting honestly and want your family's input.

Have some reassuring phrases ready, such as:

- *"I want to make sure we're all safe, and that includes me."*
- *"I'd rather bring this up now, while I have options, than wait for something serious to happen."*
- *"Your perspective matters to me, even if it's hard to hear."*

When your family responds, practice listening. Resist the urge to interrupt or defend yourself right away. Instead, reflect back what you hear: *"So you're saying you've noticed I seem more hesitant at stop signs?"* or *"It sounds like you worry when I drive in heavy traffic."* Reflective listening shows you respect their concerns, even if you don't agree with every detail.

It also helps to validate their feelings. You might say, *"I understand why this is hard—it's not easy for me either. Driving has been a big part of my life, and I know you care about me."* This keeps the conversation collaborative rather than confrontational.

By raising the subject yourself, you maintain control of the discussion. You're showing your family that you are proactive, thoughtful, and open to making adjustments when necessary. That makes it easier for them to support you, and for you to keep your independence in a safe and realistic way.

Conversation Reflection Exercise

After receiving feedback from your family, take a few minutes to reflect quietly on how the conversation went. Ask yourself: *What did I hear that was helpful? What concerns did they raise that I hadn't considered? Did anything surprise me about their perspective?* Write down your thoughts, even if they feel uncomfortable. Putting them on paper helps you sort through emotions and notice areas where you and your loved ones may actually agree.

Don't expect to resolve everything in one talk. Feedback about driving often stirs up strong feelings because it touches on independence. Instead of rushing, focus on small next steps. You might say, *"I'll pay more attention this week and see if I notice the same concerns,"* or *"After my next checkup, let's talk again with fresh information."* Agreeing on a specific follow-up—like after a doctor's appointment or in a few weeks—keeps the dialogue open and shows you're willing to listen.

By staying curious, writing down what you've heard, and revisiting the discussion with patience, you turn feedback into a tool for growth. These ongoing talks aren't about losing control—they're about building trust and ensuring that you and your loved ones feel safe and supported on the road ahead.

Responding to Family Concerns Without Conflict

It can be difficult to hear a family member express worries about your driving. Even when you know their intentions are good, their words can trigger embarrassment, frustration, or a sense of lost independence. Noticing your own challenges is hard enough—having someone else point them out can feel much worse. You may feel you must defend your ability or prove yourself again, despite many years of safe driving. These emotional reactions are natural. What matters most is handling them so they don't take over the conversation.

When you hear criticism or concern, pause before reacting. Take a slow breath and notice your body's reactions—perhaps a quickened heart rate or flushed cheeks. These are normal and simply show the topic matters to you.

Rather than letting yourself snap or argue, silently count to five, or say aloud, "I need a minute to think about what you're saying." This moment of space can make a big difference and keep conversations from escalating.

It's tempting to respond defensively, especially if your family member seems anxious or pushy. Rather than saying things like, "You don't trust me," try expressing yourself calmly: "I hear you're worried, but I'm not sure I agree right now." This approach keeps the discussion open without turning it into a confrontation. If speaking is difficult, consider writing your thoughts—a brief note or letter may help clarify your feelings and prevent misunderstandings.

It's important to set boundaries during intense or repeated conversations. You are not required to accept every suggestion or change right away. Respect-fully asserting your position builds trust. For example: "I appreciate your concern. Right now, I'll avoid night driving and stick to familiar routes." This recognizes your family's worry while setting clear, reasonable limits. These honest boundaries help everyone feel understood.

Arguments often spiral when voices rise. If tempers flare, use a physical cue—like gently raising your hand or resting your palm on the table—as a signal to pause. Calmly suggest, "Can we talk about this after dinner?" or "Let's revisit this tomorrow." Taking a break isn't avoidance; it's a sign of respect for both parties, avoiding decisions made in the heat of the moment. Even a short walk can help everyone gather their thoughts.

Family talks can drift into old stories or repeat themselves. Instead of getting pulled into past disagreements, steer things to the present: "Let's focus on what's happening now," or "I'd rather talk about what I need today." Or, redirect with questions: "What concerns you most?" or "What could help you feel safer about my driving?" Such questions show you're engaged but want a constructive conversation.

The goal of these talks is the same on both sides: safety and independence for everyone. It's helpful to state this directly: "We both want what's safest for everyone—let's work together." Let your family know you're not simply determined to keep driving, but are focused on staying active and engaged. Small compromises—like avoiding certain routes or checking in more often—can go a long way to address concerns without drastic changes.

Interactive Reflection: Practicing Calming Responses

When conversations get tense, it helps to have calming responses ready. Write out three such responses, for example:

1. "I understand why you're concerned, and I'm thinking about it."
2. "Let's pause and come back to this after we've cooled off."
3. "I'm open to making some changes and want us to keep talking about this."

Keep these on a card or by your phone as reminders during difficult discussions.

Even if a loved one seems overbearing, their worries stem from care, not control. You can maintain your dignity and preferences while understanding their point of view. Keeping discussions calm and centered on shared values, rather than personal shortcomings, increases the chance that everyone feels respected—and makes solutions easier to find for all involved.

Preparing for and Passing the DMV Road Test

Facing the DMV road test as an older adult is a unique kind of stress, but it doesn't have to be a mystery or a source of dread. Many people picture a cold, intimidating environment, but it's usually just a regular office, a waiting area with others in similar shoes, and a DMV examiner whose main goal is to keep everyone safe. These examiners have seen nervous folks of all ages. Most of them are not trying to trick you or find reasons to fail you. Their job is to ensure drivers know the rules and can handle everyday driving situations. The whole process usually takes less than an hour, from checking in at the front desk to returning from your drive. Expect a quick vision check before the road portion. Sometimes you'll sit with the examiner in your own car; other times, you might use a DMV vehicle. The examiner rides in the passenger seat, clipboard in hand, calmly giving instructions like "Turn left at the next intersection" or "Please parallel park behind that car." You may feel watched, but try to remember they want you to succeed.

Preparation starts before you set foot in the DMV. Make a checklist of what you need: your driver's license or state-issued ID, any renewal notice if you received one by mail, proof of address, and your glasses or contact lenses if you use them. Don't forget proof of insurance and registration if you'll be using your own car. I've seen people turned away for missing paperwork— double-check this list the night before. Some folks keep a folder for DMV visits so nothing slips through the cracks. It helps to lay out everything on the kitchen table before bed.

The best way to approach the road test is like any other skill: practice, repetition, and a little planning. Start by reviewing your state's driver's manual. These booklets are usually free at the DMV or available online in large print. Skim through the sections on right-of-way, school zones, roundabouts, and safe following distances. Note down anything that feels unfamiliar or confusing. Take special care with signs and markings, as these can trip up even experienced drivers if they've changed since you first learned them.

If you feel nervous about certain parts of the test, break them down into smaller steps and practice each one until it feels second nature. For example, if left turns across traffic make you anxious, spend an afternoon practicing just those at quiet intersections. If you're unsure about speed control in school zones or near playgrounds, drive those areas at off-peak hours and focus on reading and obeying every posted sign. Repetition builds muscle memory, which helps calm nerves on test day.

Anxiety is normal—almost everyone experiences jitters before a test, no matter their age or experience level. Addressing anxiety starts in the days leading up to your appointment, not just that morning. Visualize yourself arriving at the DMV, greeting the examiner with a smile, following instructions calmly, and finishing with steady hands. Positive visualization actually retrains your mind to expect success rather than failure. On the day itself, eat a light breakfast and avoid too much caffeine. Arrive early so you aren't rushing. When you park outside the DMV, take three slow breaths: inhale through your nose for a count of four, hold for two seconds, then exhale through your mouth for six counts. This slows your heartbeat and settles shaky hands. If you're waiting in line and nerves start creeping up again, focus on your feet pressing into the ground or count ceiling tiles—small distractions help keep anxiety in check.

Sometimes things don't go as planned. If you don't pass the test on your first try, it's normal to feel disappointed or embarrassed. Remind yourself that many skilled drivers need more than one attempt—failing isn't a reflection of your character or value. If this happens, ask the examiner for specific feedback on what needs improvement. Write it down if possible so nothing gets forgotten later. When talking with family afterward, honesty helps: "The examiner said I need more practice with parallel parking and checking my blind spots. I'm going to work on that before I try again." This sets a clear plan without shame or defensiveness.

If retesting feels overwhelming or if feedback suggests ongoing safety concerns that can't be quickly addressed, consider alternatives without feeling defeated. There are refresher courses for seniors—some even offer practice tests and patient instructors who know how to build confidence (AARP, n.d.). Explore other ways to stay mobile if needed; many communities offer ride services tailored to seniors who want to stay active without driving themselves.

You deserve to feel respected and supported throughout this process—not rushed or dismissed. With preparation, patience, and openness to learning new habits or skills, passing the DMV road test becomes another way to demonstrate both responsibility and determination in keeping your independence strong.

When Your Spouse Is the Driver—Supporting Each Other

Driving is often shared between partners, and the dynamics can grow complicated over time. You might notice subtle changes in your spouse's habits behind the wheel, or begin driving more yourself, quietly covering for your partner if they seem less confident. Frequently, one spouse may overlook or smooth over driving mistakes to avoid conflict. Picture a wife in the passenger seat seeing her husband roll through a stop sign—she hesitates to mention it, worried about sounding critical or hurting his feelings. Such moments create ongoing tension that can linger.

When you care for someone, you want to protect both their pride and their safety. Yet, ignoring repeat mistakes or close calls can erode trust and comfort on car rides. Instead of letting frustration simmer, view yourselves as teammates working toward mutual safety and independence for as long as possible. Addressing driving concerns with a loved one isn't easy. The key is to raise the topic gently, with patience rather than accusation—for example: "I noticed that stop sign seemed easy to miss—do you want help watching for signs, or would you prefer to focus on your own?" Framing it as teamwork softens critique and keeps you on the same side.

Some couples use these moments as opportunities for support rather than judgment. If your partner becomes flustered by directions or gets lost on familiar roads, gently ask if they want you to help with directions or reminders. "Would you like me to help with directions, or would you prefer to drive alone?" is a supportive way to offer help without taking over. Swapping roles sometimes can also help: perhaps the passenger watches traffic lights while the driver concentrates on steering. These little gestures preserve your spouse's experience while allowing you both to lean on each other.

It also helps to create a mutual agreement about handling driving changes together. Set aside a quiet time—over coffee or while doing chores—to talk about each of your needs and expectations in the car. Agree to check in regularly, like every six months, about how each feels while driving. "Let's check in every six months about driving," can encourage honest conversation before problems grow. Promise that either partner can raise driving concerns or suggest changes without blame or argument. This shared plan gives both ownership and helps prevent resentment.

Disagreements will happen. It's important to remember that compromise shows wisdom, not weakness. Maybe one wants to continue driving at night while the other worries. Rather than arguing, suggest trial changes—drive only during the day or stick to familiar routes for a month, then reassess. Sometimes, compromises need outside input: a trusted family doctor or counselor can lend perspective, and their advice often helps both partners feel heard.

Managing these challenges as a couple takes honesty, empathy, and adaptability. Covering up mistakes out of loyalty or fear only delays solutions and might risk safety. Open, honest communication—even if uncomfortable—is always the safer path. Try saying, "I know this isn't easy for either of us, but I'd rather we talk about it together than let worries build." Sometimes jotting down observations to discuss later is more productive than addressing them in the moment.

Couples' Driving Agreement Exercise

To put your intentions into practice, try making a written plan together. Ask yourselves:

- What are our "no-go" situations? (e.g., no driving after dark, no highways in bad weather)
- How often will we check in on how we each feel about driving?
- Who will help us decide if we disagree? (Doctor? Trusted family member or friend?)
- What signs will prompt us to revisit our plan? (More frequent close calls? New health conditions?)

Hang your agreement somewhere visible as a quiet reminder that you're facing these changes as partners, united in care and respect.

Building a Support Network for Safe Driving Decisions

No one should face driving decisions alone, especially when the road ahead feels less certain or a little more complicated. Community and professional resources offer more than just advice—they can provide reassurance, practical help, and sometimes, the wisdom that comes from having helped many others in similar shoes. Organizations like AARP run driver safety programs, both online and in person, that are made for older adults. These classes don't just refresh your memory about traffic laws; they can boost your confidence and introduce you to others who are also focused on staying safe behind the wheel.

AAA, another trusted resource, not only provides roadside assistance but also shares guides about car features suited for seniors, safe driving checklists, and even local workshops. Senior centers are often overlooked, yet they host transportation talks, ride-sharing signups, and practical seminars about everything from car maintenance to safe walking routes. You might find a bulletin board full of flyers about community vans, medical transport, and even volunteers happy to drive you to appointments or the store.

Sometimes your best allies are closer than you think. A neighbor who's always out gardening, a church friend who lives nearby, or even a former coworker who has flexible hours—these folks may be more than willing to help with a lift now and then. It's not always easy to ask for help, but most people feel honored when trusted with a small favor. If you offer to trade a home-cooked meal or return the favor with errands or companionship, it rarely feels like charity. Building these connections before you need them makes transitions smoother and can spark friendships that last beyond the ride.

Creating your own "safe driving team" is a wise move, not just for emergencies but as part of everyday life. Start with a simple contact list—names, phone numbers, best times to call, and notes about what each person is comfortable helping with. For instance: Pam (daughter)—rides to appointments; Ed (neighbor)—car maintenance checks; Ruth (church buddy)—backup driver for night events; local senior center—information on group outings. Keep this list somewhere easy to grab: taped to the fridge, inside your wallet, or saved in your phone with large text. If you use a cell phone, consider setting up speed dial or favorites so help is just one button away. If you prefer pen and paper, a sturdy address book with bold lettering works well. Update it as your needs change or as new people join your support circle.

The digital world can seem daunting at first, but it holds many helpful tools for seniors wanting to stay independent. Many organizations have websites where you can download printable checklists—like the ones featured in this book—for everything from pre-drive safety to emergency contacts. If you prefer print over screens, ask a friend or family member to help you print off resources or bookmark important sites on your computer or tablet. Don't be shy about asking for help saving key numbers—a grandchild or neighbor can often do this in minutes. If you like having things in hand, create a folder with copies of guides, emergency plans, and local transportation options. Some senior centers even offer tech help hours where volunteers will walk you through setting up ride-share apps or finding safe route maps for your area.

A support network is not only about having backup when things go wrong; it's about having confidence that someone is in your corner as daily routines shift. When your vision changes or you want to avoid driving in bad weather, your network fills the gap—whether that means arranging a ride to the store or having someone check your car's headlights before winter sets in. These small acts add up to peace of mind and keep you connected to your community.

11

Chapter 8: Making Your Car Work for You—Features, Maintenance, and Comfort

Adjusting Seats, Mirrors, and Pedals for Maximum Comfort

When you enter your car, comfort is essential. Cramps, stiffness, or aches before even starting to drive often signal a poor fit between you and your car. For seniors, joint stiffness can make short drives uncomfortable, but a few smart adjustments can make driving easier and safer. How you position your seat, mirrors, and pedals not only determines your comfort but affects your ability to see clearly and react quickly. If you've ended a drive with sore muscles or have trouble checking blind spots, your setup likely needs improvement.

Proper seat placement is key for both comfort and safety. The right height and distance from the pedals supports your spine, reduces fatigue, and gives a clear road view. Slide your seat forward so your knees bend comfortably with your foot on the gas; avoid stretching your leg fully or crowding your knees against the dash. Maintain about a two-finger gap between the seat edge and the back of your knee. Raise the seat so your hips are level with, or just higher than, your knees. This relieves pressure on your back and helps you see over the steering wheel without slouching. If your seat can't rise enough, use a cushion for height, but make sure all mirrors and dash displays remain visible. Recline your backrest slightly—about 100 degrees—so your spine is supported and you remain upright enough to stay alert. The headrest should align with the center of your head, improving safety in a rear-end collision.

Power seat controls make adjustments easy, letting you fine-tune height, tilt, and lumbar support. Manual levers require more effort, but the benefits are well worth it. If lumbar support is available, adjust for light pressure along your lower back, filling your spine's curve without pushing you forward—this helps prevent back pain on longer trips.

After setting your seat, adjust your mirrors. Many drivers rarely change them, but as your body and vision change, so should your mirror setup. The right mirror positioning reduces blind spots and worry. For the rearview mirror, sit in your normal position and adjust until you see as much of the rear window as possible, without changing posture. For side mirrors, use the "blind spot elimination" method: lean your head to the driver's window, adjust the left mirror to barely show your car, then lean toward the car's center and repeat with the right mirror. When seated normally, vehicles passing from behind should transition smoothly from one mirror to the next without vanishing.

Access to the pedals is another common challenge, especially for older drivers. You should press both pedals without locking your knee or needing to reach too far. If you strain to reach, check if your car has pedal adjusters or consult a mechanic about adding pedal extenders (National Highway Traffic Safety Administration, n.d.). Your heel should rest on the floor for easy pivoting between brake and gas—this improves reaction time and prevents cramps.

Interactive Element: Quick Seat & Mirror Fit Checklist

· Sit fully back in the seat; adjust until knees are slightly bent with feet on pedals.
· Raise seat so hips are at or above knee level; add a cushion if needed.
· Recline backrest just past upright (about 100 degrees).
· Set headrest so its middle is level with your head's center.
· Adjust lumbar support for gentle lower back contact.

- Adjust rearview mirror for maximum rear window visibility.
- Use the "blind spot elimination" technique for side mirrors.
- Ensure heel rests flat for easy pivot between pedals.
- Check: Can you see clearly and reach controls without strain?

Use this checklist whenever you get into a new car or after someone else has adjusted the seat. A few quick adjustments can make your drive much safer and more comfortable.

Using Modern Car Technology—Backup Cameras, Lane Assist, and More

Gone are the days when cars just had a steering wheel, pedals, and a radio— now dashboards are filled with screens and buttons, resembling a small cockpit. While these new features may seem overwhelming at first, most are designed to make driving easier and, most importantly, safer. Taking a little time to get used to them can offer real benefits behind the wheel.

Let's begin with backup cameras. For those who find reversing stressful, a backup camera simplifies the task. Shifting into reverse displays a live view of what's behind you on your dashboard screen, eliminating the guesswork and neck twisting. Colored lines on the display offer guidance: red means stop, yellow signals caution, and green means clear. To manually turn the feature on or off, look for a "camera" button or touch icon on your dashboard. If the display is unclear, check and clean the camera lens outside with a soft cloth.

Blind spot monitoring is another key advancement. Small lights or symbols appear on your side mirrors or dash when a vehicle is in your blind spot. Some systems beep gently if you attempt to change lanes while someone is there. This added "awareness" helps those with limited neck mobility. The activation button, often marked with two cars and a star or wave, can usually be found on the driver's door panel or within your car's settings. If a warning light stays on, consult your manual or your dealership.

Lane departure warning and lane assist features work to keep your car centered. If you start crossing lane lines without signaling, you might feel a vibration or hear a beep; some cars even nudge the steering slightly to keep you centered. You can turn these the assist features on or off with a button on or near the steering wheel, marked by a car between two lane lines, or through the vehicle's settings menu. Remember, these features may not operate on roads with faint or obscured lane markings—so your own vigilance is always essential.

Adaptive cruise control upgrades basic cruise control by automatically keeping a steady distance from the car ahead, adjusting speed as needed. This can greatly reduce fatigue on long trips. Set it up with the cruise control button, then use the "distance" setting (some cars show bars or car icons) to choose your preferred gap between vehicles. If you experience a loud beep, odd icon, or sudden braking, you can always tap the brakes to turn cruise control off and retake control.

Technology issues can be unnerving, with unfamiliar beeps or cryptic dashboard icons like an amber engine light or red triangle. Most manuals have a chart to decode these symbols; keeping this chart in your glove box makes it easy to check. If in doubt or if an alert won't quit, pull over safely and call your mechanic or dealership. Non-urgent alerts can generally be silenced by pressing the "OK" or "dismiss" button—just ensure you don't entirely turn off important safety features.

Real-Life Examples

Helen, once nervous about backing out of supermarket parking spaces, now relies on her backup camera to avoid bumping other cars, even on rainy days. Bill, who used to worry about blind spots, now counts on his car's blind spot monitoring to warn him before changing lanes. These technologies serve as extra safety nets for everyday drivers—not just flashy gadgets, but real aids for greater peace of mind.

Getting Additional Help

If new features still seem puzzling even after reading the manual, visit your dealership for a demonstration. Many offer free tech tutorials, especially for seniors—take notes as they walk you through the basics. Often, just a little guidance turns intimidating controls into helpful everyday tools. What was once unfamiliar quickly becomes routine, bolstering your safety and comfort each time you drive.

Adaptive Devices—Pedal Extenders, Steering Aids, and Mirror Modifications

Adaptive devices for drivers have advanced greatly, making it easier to tailor your vehicle to your mobility needs. If you have issues like stiff joints, limited reach, leg length differences, or shoulder pain, these tools can offer safer, less stressful driving. Whether you struggle with arthritis, neck motion, or leg reach, there's likely a device to help.

Pedal extenders are especially helpful if you have to stretch to reach the pedals or your knees come up too high when you move closer to the wheel. These attach directly to pedals, bringing them forward without pushing your seat uncomfortably close. Many have simple adjustment knobs for distance, and sturdy models won't slip underfoot. Before purchasing, sit in your car and measure how much closer you want the pedals—this ensures a good fit.

Steering wheel knobs assist drivers with reduced grip strength or shoulder movement. If you find sharp turns or parking maneuvers increasingly tough, a spinner knob allows smooth steering with one hand. This is ideal for those with arthritis or limited reach. Some knobs have padded or oversized handles for comfort. Try a few types at a mobility or auto parts store to find the best fit.

Mirror add-ons are life-savers if you can't turn your neck easily. Wide-angle or convex mirrors attach to your existing side mirrors, letting you see more without needing to twist. Anti-glare covers can reduce nighttime headlight discomfort. Most install easily with peel-and-stick or clip-on designs.

Seat cushions also add comfort if you sit low or have hip/back pain. Memory foam or gel options with non-slip bottoms can help you see better over the dash and prevent discomfort on longer trips.

When choosing adaptive devices, target the challenge that bothers you most—pedal extenders are great for shorter drivers or those with hip or knee issues, steering wheel knobs help with wrist or shoulder trouble, and wide-angle mirrors are for those anxious about blind spots or uncomfortable twisting around.

Installation Tips

Most devices are easy to install but require safe, secure mounting:

- *Pedal extenders*: Follow the instructions, attaching and tightening all bolts thoroughly. Test by pressing down several times—there should be no slipping or wiggling.
- *Steering wheel knobs*: Attach to a solid spot on the wheel (usually between spokes), secure all screws or clamps, and spin the knob several rotations to ensure stability.
- *Mirror add-ons*: Clean the mirror, attach the new mirror or extension as directed, and check for a secure fit.

Checklist: Safe Setup for Adaptive Devices

- Ensure the device is tightly secured—no movement under pressure
- Test the full range of motion (pedals, steering, mirrors)
- Double-check visibility and comfort
- If possible, have someone else inspect your installation
- Take a short, quiet test drive before regular use

Finding Equipment and Help

Look for reputable mobility shops that specialize in vehicle aids—ask your doctor or physical therapist for recommendations. AAA-approved garages often have experience with these installations, and larger chain auto shops may help as well (National Highway Traffic Safety Administration, n.d.). Senior centers and local aging resource lines can connect you with trusted vendors and specialists. Always select good brands and ask about return policies. When properly fitted and safely installed, adaptive devices can restore your driving comfort and put your focus back on the road, not on discomfort.

Easy Vehicle Maintenance for Seniors—A Checklist Approach

Reliable transportation starts with basic vehicle care, and you don't need to be a mechanic to keep your car safe and dependable. A few regular checks—tire pressure and tread, oil level, windshield washer fluid, and lights—are all it takes to prevent most major issues. Doing these helps reduce the risk of breakdowns and keeps your car in good shape.

Tires are your car's only contact with the road, so check them first. Underinflated tires wear quickly, lower gas mileage, and worsen braking. Each month, when tires are cold, use a digital gauge for easy reading. Find the recommended PSI in your manual or inside the driver's door. Place the gauge on the valve stem, check the number, and add air if needed. To check tread, insert a penny into the groove—if you can see the top of Lincoln's head, it's time for new tires.

Oil keeps the engine running smoothly. Check oil monthly, when the engine is cool and the car is parked level. Locate the dipstick, remove and wipe it, reinsert, then check against the marks. If oil is low or dirty, visit a drive-through oil change shop—they'll top it off fast, and are used to helping seniors.

Windshield washer fluid helps keep visibility clear. Look for the reservoir under the hood, usually with a blue or clear cap showing a wiper icon. Fill it with washer fluid (not plain water, which can freeze or breed bacteria), and check the wiper blades for cracks or splits. If wipers streak, get new ones.

Lights are crucial for safety. Each month, turn on all exterior lights: headlights, brakes, turn signals, and hazards. Ask someone to check, or look at reflections in a wall. If you spot dim or flickering bulbs, have them replaced soon.

Early trouble detection is key. Listen for odd sounds—squeaking, grinding, knocking—or note vibrations. Pay attention to dashboard warning lights: red means stop right away, yellow means check soon. Icons to know include the oil can (oil issue), battery (charging problem), and thermometer (overheating). Smoke or burning smells mean you should pull over immediately and call for help.

Here's a simple large-print checklist you can keep handy:

Monthly Maintenance Checklist

- Check tire pressure (digital gauge) and tread (penny test)
- Check oil level (dipstick)
- Top up windshield washer fluid
- Check wiper blades for cracks
- Test all exterior lights (headlights, brake lights, turn signals)
- Listen for unusual noises or vibrations
- Watch for warning lights on dashboard
- Look for leaks under the car

If bending, lifting the hood, or reading gauges is difficult, ask for help. Oil change shops often check tires and fluids for free, and some grocery store lots offer mobile maintenance vans—no appointment needed. Don't hesitate to ask a family member or neighbor for a monthly check-in—many are glad to assist.

For issues like tire bulges, persistent oil warning lights, sudden power loss, overheating, or visible leaks, call your mechanic right away; don't drive further. Keep a list of trusted auto shops in your glove box and their numbers in your phone.

Staying on top of these simple steps leads to fewer surprises on the road and more confidence when you're behind the wheel.

Choosing a Senior-Friendly Car—What to Look For

Finding the right car as a senior can seem daunting, but it's an opportunity to choose a vehicle that prioritizes your comfort, safety, and lifestyle. The ideal car should make every trip easy—avoiding unnecessary climbing, ducking, or twisting. Look for a high seating position to simplify getting in and out, and minimize bending your knees or hips. Features like wide door openings and sturdy grab handles are especially helpful if you have stiffness or balance issues. Test this by opening the car doors fully and sliding in and out on both driver and passenger sides to see how your body feels; entry and exit comfort can vary between models.

Visibility is equally important. Large windows, slim roof pillars, and a low dashboard help you see the road, curbs, and pedestrians more clearly, reducing how much you need to turn your head. Ensure the dashboard has large, readable displays and accessible buttons. If you have to squint or fumble with any controls, consider a different model. Modern vehicles usually include a backup camera, but also look for features like blind spot indicators, straightforward climate controls, and bright, easy-to-read gauges.

A proper test drive means more than a quick trip around the block. Set aside time to really get to know the vehicle: adjust the seat and mirrors, and test every lever, dial, and button to make sure they're easy to reach and operate. Try common tasks—change the radio, activate the wipers, open storage compartments. Get in and out multiple times and check the comfort of every seat to ensure it suits both you and your regular passengers. Practice parking and backing up using mirrors and cameras to assess your comfort with the car's visibility and turning radius.

Deciding between new and used cars often comes down to budget. Newer models come with the latest safety technology—like automatic emergency braking and cross-traffic alerts—but at a higher price. If you drive often, especially in city traffic, these features may be worth the investment for added safety. Certified pre-owned cars are a good compromise; they're inspected by the manufacturer, come with extended warranties, and offer many modern features at a lower cost than brand new models.

Cost is a key consideration. A gently used car, two or three years old from a reputable dealer, can offer excellent value without paying for unnecessary extras. Factor in the full cost of ownership: insurance, maintenance, and fuel economy should all be compared before buying. If possible, bring a trusted friend or family member to help spot any issues during the test drive or negotiations.

Use reliable resources dedicated to senior drivers for car recommendations. Guides from AARP focus on comfort, safety, and accessibility, prioritizing real-world usability over flashy features. Kelley Blue Book and Consumer Reports also offer detailed reviews of cars favored for entry height, seating, visibility, and dashboard simplicity. Models frequently recommended include:

- **Subaru Forester**—noted for its high seating and wide doors
- **Honda CR-V**—praised for reliability and easy-to-use controls
- **Toyota Camry**—known for its comfort and smooth ride
- **Ford Escape**—appreciated for manageable size and intuitive dashboard

When narrowing down your choices, review automaker websites for interior photos and feature lists. Bring a printed checklist to the dealership to take notes and compare vehicles easily. Take your time, and don't feel pressured by sales staff—this decision impacts your comfort and safety for years to come. Ask questions about every control and feature until you feel entirely at ease. Above all, remember: it's your car, your independence, and your peace of mind on the road.

Getting Help with Upkeep—Finding Trustworthy Mechanics and Services

Car care goes beyond oil changes and tires—it's also about finding mechanics you trust and knowing how to communicate your needs. Many older adults have experienced unreliable service or confusing repair shops, but you deserve better. A great way to start is by asking neighbors, friends at your senior center, or fellow church members for recommendations. Mechanics who have earned a good reputation usually keep it for a reason.

Look for shops with ASE certification, indicated by a blue or white seal. This means the technicians are tested and up-to-date with new technology. Clean, organized shops with staff who patiently answer questions also tend to be more reliable.

Watch for red flags such as pushy sales tactics, vague estimates, or impatience when you ask for details. If a mechanic dismisses your concerns, refuses written estimates, or won't explain issues plainly, find someone else. Always request, "Could you write down exactly what needs fixing and how much it will cost?" and expect a call before extra work is done. A reputable mechanic will gladly explain repairs in simple terms and show you broken parts if you ask.

Be clear about your needs and accessibility upfront. Try simple phrases like, "Can you explain the problem in everyday words?" or "Could you write out what you did and circle anything I should monitor?" If walking a large lot is hard or you need help getting to your car, just ask. "Could someone walk me out to my car when it's ready?" is a perfectly fair request. If you use a mobility device or have specific health concerns, be upfront—good shops are happy to accommodate.

Community services can make car care easier. Many senior centers host "car check" days with trusted mechanics who check fluids, tires, and lights for free or at low cost. Some towns offer mobile mechanics who come to your home—ideal if getting out is hard. Your Area Agency on Aging or the senior center bulletin board may list these resources. Certain AAA chapters also have shop recommendations for older adults.

Interactive Element: Car Care Conversation Starters

- List two people you know who trust their mechanics. Write their names and contact info.
- Bring this prompt to the shop: "Please explain what repairs are needed in plain English."
- Schedule your next oil change reminder on your phone or calendar.
- Have your car buddy touch base after long trips or season changes.

With these steps, you'll take control of your car's upkeep and feel confident that both your vehicle and your mechanic are working in your best interest.

12

Chapter 9: Exploring Independence Beyond the Driver's Seat

Senior Ride Programs and Community Shuttles—How to Get Started

Picture this: it's a sunny Thursday and you'd like to see a movie or head to a doctor's appointment, but no family or friends are available to give you a ride. That's where senior ride programs and community shuttles step in. They're designed specifically to help older adults stay mobile, independent, and connected without relying solely on loved ones. These services are more than just backup transportation—they're tools that help you keep your freedom.

Many of these programs are offered through local agencies, nonprofits, churches, or even hospitals. Their main goal is to ensure seniors don't miss medical visits, essential errands, or opportunities to stay socially active. Often, eligibility starts at age 60 or 65, though some programs accept anyone who has difficulty driving. Common providers include your county's Area Agency on Aging, local senior centers, and faith-based organizations. Some medical centers provide transportation for patients needing regular treatment, and volunteer programs are available too, where neighbors drive for a small fee or donation.

If you're unsure where to start, your local senior center is often the best first stop—they usually maintain an updated list of transportation providers. Another helpful tool is the Eldercare Locator (eldercare.acl.gov), a government website where you can enter your zip code to find senior ride options nearby. Be ready to share your address and note any mobility needs, like using a walker or wheelchair. When calling, ask about eligibility requirements, service areas, and the costs involved.

Most programs require a quick registration process. This may include filling out a form with your emergency contacts, mobility needs, and regular destinations. Some programs will help you register by phone if paperwork is difficult. Once you're registered, rides are typically scheduled by calling 24–48 hours ahead, though many allow recurring reservations for weekly trips like grocery shopping or medical treatments.

These rides are usually designed to be as convenient as possible. Many programs offer door-to-door service, meaning the driver will help you from your front door to the car and then to the entrance of your destination. Others provide curb-to-curb service, so be sure to clarify which applies. If you need assistance with bags, steps, or mobility aids, mention this when scheduling so the program can send a driver equipped to help.

Instead of a set pickup time, you'll often be given a pickup window, since drivers may be serving multiple passengers on the same route. Flexibility helps, especially during busy hours or bad weather. If you know you'll need extra time to get ready, let the dispatcher know when you call.

Safety is a top priority. Drivers usually go through background checks and are trained to assist seniors. Vehicles are regularly inspected and many programs have wheelchair-accessible vans available upon request.

As for cost, these services are generally affordable—far less than taxis or private ride services. Some operate on donations, while others charge a small fee per ride (often between $2 and $5). Grants, church support, or community funding often help keep costs low, and financial assistance may be available if needed.

If you find a driver you enjoy riding with, some programs allow you to request them again for future trips. This adds familiarity and comfort, turning transportation into a pleasant routine instead of a source of stress.

Interactive Element: Quick-Start Ride Service Checklist

- List three local programs using information from your senior center or the Eldercare Locator.
- Call each and ask:
- What are the eligibility rules?
- How far do they travel?
- Do they offer door-to-door service?
- Are vehicles wheelchair accessible?
- What does each ride cost?
- Register with at least one provider this week—even if you don't need a ride yet—so you're prepared.
- Schedule a practice ride (such as to lunch with friends) to familiarize yourself with the process before an urgent need arises.

By signing up for senior ride programs and community shuttles, you keep control over your mobility. Making these services part of your routine can make every outing—from Sunday services to pharmacy trips or coffee with friends—simpler and less stressful (Senior Services of America, n.d.).

Using Uber, Lyft, and Ride Apps—A Step-by-Step Visual Guide

Getting around town no longer means waiting for a taxi or depending on someone else's schedule. Apps like Uber and Lyft have changed how people of all ages travel, but if you haven't used them before, these digital tools can seem mysterious or even intimidating. I want to walk you through the process in a way that makes it feel less like learning a new language and more like picking up the phone to call a friend. The first step is to get the app onto your smartphone or tablet. If you have an iPhone, you'll need to open the App Store; for Android phones, use the Google Play Store. Type "Uber" or "Lyft" in the search bar, then tap the button marked "Get" or "Install." The app will download quickly—usually in less than a minute if your internet is working well. Once it's finished, find the new icon on your home screen and tap it to open.

Setting up your account is next. The app will ask for your name, phone number, and a way to pay—credit card, debit card, or sometimes PayPal. You'll create a password that's easy for you to remember but hard for others to guess. Try something unique, add a number or symbol, and write it down somewhere safe if you need to. Don't worry; reputable rideshare apps use heavy encryption and don't share your payment information with drivers. You'll only need to enter this once, and after that, payments happen automatically after each ride.

When it's time to book a ride, the app's home screen shows a simple map with a blinking dot for your location. At the top, there's a space that says "Where to?" Tap it and type in where you want to go—maybe the grocery store, your doctor's office, or your granddaughter's house. You can either enter an address or choose from saved favorites if you visit the same places often. After that, the app will show you different ride choices: standard (often called UberX or Lyft), larger vehicles if friends are joining, or sometimes options with wheelchair access. Pick the one that fits your needs. You'll see an estimated cost before you confirm.

Once you request a ride, the app shows you your driver's name, photo, and what kind of car they're driving—including the license plate number. Don't rush outside right away—wait until the app says the driver is close by or has arrived. When the car pulls up, always check that the license plate and car model match what's on your screen. Ask the driver their name before getting in, and let them confirm yours too. This is a normal safety step; drivers expect it.

The ride itself is usually smooth and direct. If you want family to know where you are, tap "Share My Trip" on the screen. This sends a live map to someone you trust so they can see where you are in real time. The app also has an emergency button—if anything makes you uncomfortable, press it to quickly connect with help.

Tipping is easy and electronic. After your ride ends, the app asks if you'd like to add a tip for your driver—usually a few dollars or whatever feels right for good service. You don't need cash; just tap an amount on the screen and it adds to your total.

Sometimes things don't go as planned—a driver might be delayed by traffic or cancel at the last minute. If this happens, the app will either find you another driver automatically or give you the option to book again. If you run into issues, there's always a help button in the app; you can write a quick note and usually get a reply within an hour or two.

A few questions come up again and again: What if I have mobility aids? Most drivers are happy to help stow walkers or fold up small wheelchairs—just mention it when you book by using the notes section or calling your driver through the app once matched. What about cost? Prices change based on distance and time of day, but you always see an estimate before confirming. If you're worried about spending too much, wait until the fare drops or pick a less expensive ride option.

If you're new to smartphone technology, ask a family member or friend to walk through these steps with you the first time. Many local libraries and senior centers offer free classes or one-on-one coaching for apps like Uber and Lyft. Don't let embarrassment stop you from asking for help; everyone starts as a beginner.

Navigating Public Transit with Ease and Confidence

For many older adults, buses and trains are more than just a way to get from one place to another—they're a lifeline for staying independent, saving money, and keeping social connections strong. Public transit can take you to a doctor's appointment, a senior center gathering, or even a favorite park, all without the stress of driving or parking. One of the biggest advantages is affordability. Most transit systems offer reduced fares or free passes for seniors, often beginning at age 65 or with proof of Medicare. With discounted rates, it's possible to stretch your budget while still enjoying the freedom of getting out and about.

Accessibility has come a long way in recent years. Modern buses often lower to meet sidewalk level, with ramps for walkers or wheelchairs and wide doors for easier entry. Priority seating near the driver is reserved for seniors and those with mobility needs, and drivers are trained to wait until passengers are seated before pulling away. Many train systems also offer step-free boarding, wide aisles, and large-print signage to make travel smoother. While challenges like crowded vehicles or confusing transfer points still exist, planning ahead helps reduce stress and makes transit a viable, comfortable option.

Planning your trip is easier than ever. Many transit agencies provide online trip planners—just type in where you are and where you want to go, and you'll receive a detailed itinerary with times and transfer points. If you prefer paper, most libraries, city halls, or senior centers carry printed schedules with route numbers and stops clearly listed. Highlight your starting point and destination for quick reference. If you'd rather speak to a person, call the agency's customer service line. Representatives can walk you through options, answer questions, and give you tips about transfers.

When heading out, give yourself extra time to reach your stop. Wear comfortable shoes and, if needed, carry a small folding seat or cushion. Check the route number on the front of the bus or train, and don't hesitate to ask the driver for confirmation. Drivers are accustomed to helping seniors and will usually lower the ramp or give you extra time to board if you ask.

Hold onto rails or straps while walking down the aisle, and keep canes or walkers close but out of pathways. Place bags at your feet or on your lap to avoid blocking others. When your stop is near, press the "stop" button or pull the cord, and wait until the vehicle has fully stopped before gathering your belongings.

If you're new to transit or feel uneasy, start small. Ride with a friend or family member on your first trip, or practice on familiar, short routes before trying longer ones. Some cities offer "travel ambassador" or buddy programs that pair seniors with volunteers who ride along until you feel confident. You can also use tools like Google Street View to preview transfer stops or write step-by-step instructions on a notecard to carry in your wallet.

Letting the driver know your destination can be especially reassuring—they often give a friendly reminder when it's time to get off. If you make a mistake or miss a stop, remember it happens to everyone. Carry a small amount of cash, a prepaid fare card, and a list of important phone numbers for backup.

Public transit doesn't have to feel intimidating. With each successful ride, you build both confidence and competence, turning buses and trains into reliable, stress-free tools for staying connected. Over time, using transit may feel as natural as driving once did—offering freedom, flexibility, and the peace of mind that comes with knowing you can get where you want to go safely and independently.

Staying Social and Active Without a Car

Losing the keys doesn't mean losing your connection to the world. In fact, stepping away from driving can open doors you may not have considered. Instead of focusing on what's left behind—the car in the garage, the familiar routes, the habit of hopping behind the wheel—think of it as an opportunity to gain more. More time for friends. More energy for your favorite activities. More chances to explore new places and connect with people in new ways. Imagine taking a community shuttle to your weekly card game at the senior center. Instead of stressing about parking or traffic, you're laughing with friends on the ride over, swapping stories, maybe even learning a new trick at the table. A small change in how you get there can make a big difference in how connected you feel.

There are countless ways to stay active without a car. Local book clubs often meet near bus stops or offer carpools, making it easy to join lively discussions without worrying about nighttime driving or bad weather. Senior centers are full of activities like yoga, painting, movie nights, and technology workshops— and many provide shuttles right to their doors. Faith communities also play a big role, organizing study groups, potlucks, and special events. Even if you can't drive, someone is almost always willing to give you a lift so you never miss Sunday lunch or choir practice.

Volunteering is another powerful way to stay engaged without needing your own set of wheels. Food banks, animal shelters, libraries, and hospitals often welcome seniors who arrive by bus, shuttle, or carpool. Whether you're sorting donations, reading to children, or lending a hand at community events, volunteering strengthens your sense of purpose while expanding your social circle. Many organizations even coordinate rides for volunteers, so don't hesitate to ask about transportation when signing up.

If you enjoy bringing people together, you might consider starting a neighborhood carpool or ride-share group. This is about more than transportation—it's about community. Reach out to a few friends or neighbors and suggest rotating driving duties for shopping, medical appointments, or social outings. A simple suggestion like, "We both shop on Thursdays—why don't we take turns driving?" can spark a system that eases the burden for everyone. Establishing a shared schedule—like Mondays for errands with one neighbor and Fridays for the farmer's market with another—keeps things organized and dependable. Flexibility is key; if someone isn't comfortable driving at night or in bad weather, adjust plans together.

The benefits of staying socially active reach far beyond convenience. Time with others can boost your mood, sharpen your memory, and even improve overall health. Studies consistently show that seniors who join group activities, volunteer, or see friends regularly are less likely to feel lonely or depressed. They also tend to report sharper minds and greater day-to-day happiness. Evelyn, a woman I once met on a knitting club shuttle, told me that after she gave up driving, she actually made more friends than before. The rides themselves became part of the fun, with conversations that left her feeling connected and optimistic.

Even if arranging outings without a car feels unfamiliar at first, every new experience builds confidence. Try a painting class across town, a community gardening workshop, or a local bingo night. If you're unsure about going alone, invite a friend or neighbor—it's often easier when you know someone will be there with you. Many groups intentionally make participation accessible for all, listing "near public transit" on flyers or offering carpools. Calling ahead to ask about ride options is another great way to ensure you won't be left out.

True independence isn't tied to driving—it's tied to choice. It's about deciding how you want to spend your time and with whom. Shifting away from driving doesn't shrink your world; it expands it. You might discover new activities, deepen connections with neighbors, and make friendships in unexpected places. The world outside your door is still full of opportunity— and often, it's just one ride away..

Building Your Personal Transportation Plan for the Future

There comes a point when planning ahead for mobility isn't just wise—it's a gift to yourself and to those who care about you. Maybe certain errands or appointments are starting to feel like more of a chore, or you've caught yourself wondering how you'll get around if driving becomes less comfortable. The truth is, the sooner you sketch out a plan, the more options you'll have and the less stress you'll face later. This isn't about giving up your independence or expecting the worst. It's about creating choices, peace of mind, and the confidence to stay active on your own terms.

Start simple, with a blank sheet of paper or worksheet. On one side, list every transportation option you know in your area. Begin with family or friends who might offer occasional rides. Add local shuttles, senior ride programs, taxi companies, ride apps you're comfortable with, and nearby public transit lines. Don't overlook neighbors who might be open to carpooling for shopping, or community groups like churches, the Lions Club, or Rotary—many have volunteer drivers who help with short trips.

Next, write down your usual destinations. Think about your weekly and monthly routines—grocery store, pharmacy, hair salon, doctor's office, or maybe your grandchild's soccer field. Create a second column for these destinations and draw lines connecting them to the services that can get you there. This exercise makes it easy to see where you're covered and where you may need backup. For example, your senior shuttle may stop service at 4 p.m., but a neighbor does grocery runs in the evening and wouldn't mind company. Or maybe public transit works well on weekdays but not weekends, making ride apps or family rides more valuable for Sunday outings.

Flexibility is key. No single service has to cover everything. Mix and match what works best: use shuttles for medical appointments, carpools for shopping, and ride apps for last-minute plans. If you're comfortable with color-coding or symbols, add them to your list so you can see at a glance which option works for each destination. Keep your plan handy—in your purse, on the fridge, or next to the phone—so you're never scrambling when you need a ride.

Don't build this plan alone. Involve family, caregivers, or close friends. Share your list with them—whether as a printed copy or over the phone—so they know your preferences and can help when needed. If loved ones live far away, schedule regular check-ins by phone or video chat to review your plan together. Services change, and so do health needs, so set reminders to revisit your plan every few months. A quick update can make sure your list stays current and useful.

It's normal to feel mixed emotions while doing this. You may feel frustrated about not being able to drive everywhere or relieved to see that there are more options than you realized. Both reactions are completely valid. Some people even discover new resources during this process and share them with friends or family, turning their plan into a tool for the whole community.

The strength of a personal transportation plan is in its flexibility. It doesn't have to be perfect. Cross off services that no longer fit your needs, and add new ones as they become available. Update it as often as life requires. The goal isn't just mobility—it's confidence, control, and the assurance that you'll always have a way to stay connected to the people and places that matter most.

Worksheet: Mapping Out Your Transportation Plan

- Write down all family, friends, and neighbors willing to help with rides.
- List each transportation service available—shuttles, ride apps, taxis, carpools.
- For each regular destination (doctor, store, social gathering), note which options cover it.
- Identify any gaps (times/days/places) and brainstorm creative ways to fill them.
- Share this worksheet with family or caregivers; discuss updates every few months.

· Post it where it's easy to find (fridge, front hall, notebook).

When you take time now to create and maintain this plan, you protect your independence and reduce anxiety about the future. It means more freedom—not less—since you know how to get where you want to go even if circumstances shift unexpectedly.

A little planning today goes a long way toward keeping life full of activity and meaningful connections tomorrow. The next chapter will show how building safer habits and routines can help you keep enjoying the ride—no matter which seat you're sitting in.

13

Conclusion

If you've made it to this final chapter, I want to pause and say thank you. You've stuck with me through stories, checklists, routines, and more than a few honest conversations about change. That takes courage. And it shows a truth I've witnessed again and again working with seniors—you have more resilience and adaptability than you may realize.

Let's be clear: this book was never meant to take your keys or independence. Quite the opposite. My goal has always been to help you drive longer, safer, and with more confidence. I believe, deeply, that independence isn't tied to the act of driving itself. It's about having the freedom to make choices, to stay connected, and to keep setting your own course—on the road and in life.

Here's what we've covered together. We started by looking at how aging can affect driving—changes in vision, hearing, reflexes, and even how your body handles medications. We talked about the value of honest self-reflection and the strength it takes to notice changes and act on them, rather than ignoring or hiding them away. We broke down the nuts and bolts of planning safe trips: picking the right time, mapping out easier routes, and preparing for the curveballs that weather, traffic, or even a tricky parking lot can throw your way.

We explored how to stay sharp and alert behind the wheel—getting enough rest, managing distractions, and using mindful habits to keep your attention on the present moment. I shared practical routines for scanning mirrors, recognizing drowsiness, and knowing when it's time to pull over and regroup. We didn't shy away from the tough stuff, either: handling intersections, merging, freeways, glare, and even snow or rain. These aren't just tips— they're tools you can use to turn anxiety into action.

We talked about recognizing when driving needs to change, not as a loss, but as an act of responsibility and self-respect. Together, we practiced using self-assessment checklists—not to judge, but to help you notice patterns and feel in control. We looked at how to talk with family and friends, how to take feedback to heart, and how to prepare for DMV renewals or road tests with your dignity intact.

This guide also covered the practical side of keeping your car comfortable and safe: adjusting seats and mirrors, using new vehicle technology, and knowing which features make a car truly "senior-friendly." We looked at easy maintenance routines and how to find mechanics you can trust. And when driving no longer feels right or safe, we explored alternative ways to stay mobile—senior shuttles, ride apps, public transit, and community carpools.

Let me highlight what I hope you'll take away most:

· Use the self-assessment tools and checklists. They're not just for today. Keep them close. Review them every few months or after any close call.

· Try adaptive driving strategies—adjust your routine, your vehicle, or your routes. Small tweaks can make a huge difference.

· Communicate openly with your circle. Ask family or friends to ride along, give feedback, or help with new technology.

· Don't shy away from new car features. Backup cameras, lane assist, and blind spot monitors exist to help you—not to confuse you. If you need a demonstration, ask for one.

· Plan for the future. A written transportation plan is a gift to yourself and those who care about you. It keeps you in the driver's seat, even if you're riding in the passenger seat.

Your willingness to learn, to adapt, and to face challenges head-on is worth celebrating. I know from experience that many people your age feel pressure to "prove" themselves on the road or worry about judgment from others. But every time you pause to reflect, ask for help, or try something new, you're showing strength—not weakness. You're taking charge of your safety and your freedom.

Here's my call to action for you: Don't let this book gather dust. Keep it in your glove compartment, on the kitchen table, or wherever you'll see it often. Before a trip, review the checklists. When you get a new car or try a new route, revisit the routines. If you're having a tough conversation with family, use the sample scripts. And if you're ready for something new, check the resource section for senior ride programs, car adaptation services, and refresher courses from organizations like AARP and AAA.

And don't keep what you've learned to yourself. Share these tools with your spouse, friends, or neighbors. Talk about your routines and safety plans. Invite others to join you in a refresher course or try out a new rideshare app together. The more we support each other, the safer and more connected our communities become.

I know change isn't always easy. I've seen the mix of pride and vulnerability that comes with every stage of the driving journey. But I also know that knowledge, preparation, and support can turn uncertainty into confidence. With each new habit, each honest conversation, and each careful adjustment, you're building a safer, more independent future—not just for yourself, but for everyone who shares the road with you.

So here's to you—your wisdom, your grit, and your desire to keep moving forward. The road ahead may change, but your ability to adapt, connect, and thrive remains as strong as ever.

Let's keep the journey going—safely, confidently, and together.

One last favor: if this book has helped you, please consider leaving a review. Even a few sentences go a long way in helping other readers discover this guide and benefit from it just as you have. Your review could be the reason someone else finds the tools they need to keep driving safely and independently.

14

References

- *Driving Independence and Mental Health for Seniors* https://drivingtoindep endence.com/driving-independence-mental-health-seniors/
- *Physical Activity Benefits for Adults 65 or Older* https://www.cdc.gov/physic al-activity-basics/health-benefits/older-adults.html
- *Understanding driving anxiety in older adults* https://pubmed.ncbi.nlm.nih. gov/30415755/
- *Community Stories* https://cluballiance.aaa.com/the-extra-mile/connect/ Community-Stories
- *Safe Driving for Older Adults | National Institute on Aging* https://www.nia.ni h.gov/health/safety/safe-driving-older-adults
- *Driving Aids for Arthritis: Benefits and Recommendations* https://www.mobi lityinmotion.com/driving-aids-for-arthritis-how-they-work-and-whi ch-are-best-for-you/
- *Some Medicines and Driving Don't Mix* https://www.fda.gov/consumers/co nsumer-updates/some-medicines-and-driving-dont-mix
- *Evaluate Your Driving Ability - AAA Exchange* https://exchange.aaa.com/saf ety/senior-driver-safety-mobility/evaluate-your-driving-ability/#:~:te xt=Drivers%2065%20Plus%20is%20a,information%20about%20your% 20driving%20performance.
- *5 Tips for Older Drivers Planning a Road Trip* https://www.ace.aaa.com/auto

motive/advocacy/older-drivers-road-trip-tips.html
- *The Best Navigation Apps for 2025* https://www.pcmag.com/picks/the-best
  -navigation-apps
- *Retiree travel checklist* https://blog.withfaye.com/travel-checklists/retiree
  -travel-checklist/
- *Understanding Older Drivers: An Examination of Medical ...* https://aaafound
  ation.org/understanding-older-drivers-examination-medical-conditio
  ns-medication-use-travel-behavior/
- *Age-Related Effect of Sleepiness on Driving Performance* https://pmc.ncbi.nl
  m.nih.gov/articles/PMC8393523/
- *The Older Driver - Older People's Health Issues* https://www.msdmanuals.co
  m/home/older-people-s-health-issues/the-older-driver/the-older-dri
  ver
- *Mindfulness and Stress-Reduction Techniques for Drivers* https://drivingtoin
  dependence.com/mindfulness-stress-reduction-techniques-drivers/
- *Tip Sheet: Safety Tips for Older Drivers* https://www.healthinaging.org/tool
  s-and-tips/tip-sheet-safety-tips-older-drivers
- *Driving Safely While Aging Gracefully* https://www.nhtsa.gov/older-drivers
  /driving-safely-while-aging-gracefully
- *Vision and night driving abilities of elderly drivers* https://pubmed.ncbi.nlm.
  nih.gov/23683029/
- *Safe Driving for Older Adults | National Institute on Aging* https://www.nia.ni
  h.gov/health/safety/safe-driving-older-adults
- *Preventing Parking Lot Tragedies Involving Older Adults* https://compassion
  atetransitions.org/blog/f/preventing-parking-lot-tragedies-involving-
  older-adults
- *When to be Concerned About a Senior Driver | Via* https://mwg.aaa.com/via/
  car/unsafe-driver-warning-signs
- *Evaluate Your Driving Ability* https://exchange.aaa.com/safety/senior-driv
  er-safety-mobility/evaluate-your-driving-ability/
- *Aging Parents and Driving: How & When To approach the ...* https://seniorser
  vicesofamerica.com/blog/aging-parents-and-driving/
- *Driving Laws for Older Drivers by State* https://lifelanes.progressive.com/se

nior-driving-laws-by-state/

- *Safe Driving for Older Adults | National Institute on Aging* https://www.nia.ni h.gov/health/safety/safe-driving-older-adults
- *AARP Driver Safety: Online and Classroom Courses* https://www.aarp.org/au to/driver-safety/
- *Taking the Keys Away From an Elderly Driver* https://www.ourparents.com/ senior-health/what-to-do-when-its-time-for-your-parents-to-stop-driving
- *Driving Safely While Aging Gracefully* https://www.nhtsa.gov/older-drivers /driving-safely-while-aging-gracefully
- *The Best Cars for Seniors, All the Features You Need* https://www.kbb.com/b est-cars/seniors/
- *How to Adjust Seating to the Proper Position While Driving* https://www.wiki how.com/Adjust-Seating-to-the-Proper-Position-While-Driving
- *Adapted Vehicles* https://www.nhtsa.gov/vehicle-safety/adapted-vehicles
- *Car Buying Resources to Help You Get the Best Deal* https://www.aarp.org/au to/car-buying/
- *Transportation - Eldercare Locator - ACL.gov* https://eldercare.acl.gov/publ ic/resources/topic/Transportation.aspx
- *How to Use Uber for Seniors: A Simple Guide for Safe Rides* https://seniorsite. org/resource/how-to-use-uber-for-seniors-a-simple-guide-for-safe-rides/
- *Transport for Elderly People: A Guide to Safe & Accessible ...* https://12oaks.ne t/transport-for-elderly-people/
- *What Are the Options for Senior Transportation?* https://seniorservicesofam erica.com/blog/what-are-the-options-for-senior-transportation/